NATEF Correlated Task Sheets

for

AUTOMOTIVE MAINTENANCE AND LIGHT REPAIR

James D. Halderman

Boston   Columbus   Indianapolis   New York   San Francisco   Upper Saddle River
Amsterdam   Cape Town   Dubai   London   Madrid   Milan   Munich   Paris   Montréal   Toronto
Delhi   Mexico City   São Paulo   Sydney   Hong Kong   Seoul   Singapore   Taipei   Tokyo

Vice President and Executive Publisher: Vernon Anthony
Senior Acquisitions Editor: Lindsey Prudhomme Gill
Editorial Assistant: Amanda Cerreto
Director of Marketing: David Gesell
Marketing Manager: Harper Coles
Senior Marketing Coordinator: Alicia Wozniak
Production Manager: Holly Shufeldt
Cover Designer: George Jacobs, Integra Software Services, Ltd.
Full-Service Project Management/Composition: Abinaya Rajendran,
  Integra Software Services, Ltd.
Printer/Binder: Edwards Brothers Malloy

10 9 8 7 6 5 4 3 2 1

ISBN-13: 978-0-13-344430-8
ISBN-10:   0-13-344430-9

CONTENTS

Chapter 12-Measuring Systems and Tools

Chapter 13-Service Information

Chapter 14-Vehicle Identification and Emission Ratings

Chapter 15-Gasoline Engine Operation

Chapter 16-Diesel Engine Operation

Chapter 17-Under Hood Inspection

Chapter 18-Lube, Oil, and Filter Service

Chapter 19-Engine Cooling System

Chapter 20-Engine Condition Diagnosis

Chapter 21-In-Vehicle Engine Service

Chapter 22-Gaskets and Sealants

Chapter 23-Electrical Fundamentals

Chapter 24-Electrical Circuits

Chapter 25-Series, Parallel, and Series-Parallel Circuits

Chapter 26-Circuit Testers and Digital Meters

vi

Vehicle Chassis Identification

Meets NATEF Task: (A4-A-4) Locate and interpret vehicle identification numbers. (P-1)

Name _____ Date _____

Make/Model _____ Year _____ Instructor's OK [ ]

_____ 1. From observations or by checking service information, determine the type of body

construction (check all that apply)

_____ Full frame

_____ Stub frame

_____ Unit body

_____ Other (describe) _____

_____ 2. FWD or RWD? _____

_____ 3. List the major components of the drivetrain:

_____

_____

_____

_____ 4. Type of suspension (describe): _____

_____

_____ 5. Type of steering system (describe): _____

_____

Vehicle Service Facility Visit

Meets NATEF Task: Not specified by NATEF

Name _____ **Date** _____

Make/Model _____ **Year** _____ **Instructor's OK** [ ]

_____ **1.** Visit a local vehicle repair facility. Date of visit: _____

_____ **2.** Check the type of facility visited:

        _____ Independent garage

        _____ New vehicle dealership

        _____ State, county, or local fleet garage

        _____ Specialty shop

        _____ Mass merchandiser

        _____ Other (describe) _____

_____ **3.** How many service technicians work at this facility?

        _____ 1-3 _____ 4-6 _____ more than 6

_____ **4.** Are uniforms/laundry paid for? _____ Yes _____ No

_____ **5.** What is the pay method?

        _____ Flat-rate _____ Salary

        _____ Hourly _____ Other (describe) _____

_____ **6.** What are the hours of operation? _____

_____ **7.** Does the service facility pay for certification tests? _____ Yes _____ No

_____ **8.** List the name and title of the person you visited.

        Name _____ Title _____

Sample Resume

Meets NATEF Task: Not specified by NATEF

Name _____ **Date** _____

Make/Model _____ **Year** _____ **Instructor's OK** [ ]

_____ **1.** Write below a sample resume, including all needed and important information about your talents, skills, education, and training.

_____

_____

_____

_____

_____

_____

_____

_____

_____

_____

_____

_____

_____

_____ **2.** Instructor's comments and/or suggestions for improvement. _____

_____

_____

Sample Cover Letter

Meets NATEF Task: Not specified by NATEF

Name _____ Date _____

Make/Model _____ Year _____ Instructor's OK [　　]

_____ 1. Write below a sample cover letter that would be used to accompany your resume

when applying for a job.

_____

_____

_____

_____

_____

_____

_____

_____

_____

_____

_____

_____

_____ 2. Instructor's comments and/or suggestions for improvement. _____

_____

_____

Job Shadowing

Meets NATEF Task: Not specified by NATEF

Name _____ Date _____

Make/Model _____ Year _____ Instructor's OK [   ]

_____ 1. List the name and address of the shop or dealership where job shadowing occurred,

the date, and time spent:

Name _____ Date: _____

Address _____ Time: _____

_____

Telephone _____

_____ 2. List the name and title of the person who was being shadowed:

Name _____

Title _____

_____ 3. What part of the jobs being performed interested you the most? _____

_____

Why? _____

_____ 4. What part of the jobs being performed did not appeal to you? _____

_____

Why? _____

_____ 5. Based on the job shadowing experience, is the type of job of interest enough to be

considered a future career? _____

_____

Work Order

Meets NATEF Task: (A8-A-1) Complete work order and complete necessary customer and vehicle information. (P-1)

Name _____ **Date** _____

Make/Model _____ **Year** _____ **Instructor's OK** [　　]

_____ 1. List the items about the **vehicle** that should be included on the work order (also called a repair order - R.O).

      a. _____   e. _____

      b. _____   f. _____

      c. _____   g. _____

      d. _____   h. _____

_____ 2. List the information about the **driver/owner** that should be included on the work order.

      a. _____

      b. _____

      c. _____

      d. _____

_____ 3. List the three Cs (concern, cause, and correction) that the service technician should write on the work order for a repair that includes a diagnosis of the problem (concern), the replacement of a part, and the verification of the repair.

      a. _____

      b. _____

      c. _____

7

ASE Technician Certification

Meets NATEF Task: Not specified by NATEF

Name _____ **Date** _____

Make/Model _____ **Year** _____ **Instructor's OK** [ ]

_____ **1.** Check the ASE web site (www.ase.com) and answer the following questions:

    a. How many years of hand-on experience is needed? _____

    b. What types of questions are asked? _____

    _____

    c. How many ASE test areas are there? _____

    d. What must be passed to become a master technician? _____

_____ **2.** Print out the ASE test task list and check all areas where more study or experience is

needed. (Show this to your instructor.) List the areas of most concern:

_____

_____

_____

_____

_____

Instructor's Check Off _____

8

Shop Safety Checklist

Meets NATEF Task: Not specified by NATEF

Name _____ **Date** _____

Make/Model _____ **Year** _____ **Instructor's OK** [　　]

_____ **1.** Walk through the shop(s) area of the school or a local shop or dealership and check for the following items:

      a. Shields on bench or pedestal grinders   Yes___ No___ NA___

      b. Exhaust hoses in good repair   Yes___ No___ NA___

      c. Fire extinguisher installed and charged   Yes___ No___ NA___

      d. First aid kit visible and fully stocked   Yes___ No___ NA___

      e. Fire blanket visible and useable   Yes___ No___ NA___

      f. Eye wash station visible and usable   Yes___ No___ NA___

_____ **2.** List anything that should be included in a safe shop that was not present.

      _____

      _____

_____ **3.** What items of personal protective equipment were being worn by service technicians?

      a. Safety glasses/face shield   Yes___ No___ NA___

      b. Protective gloves   Yes___ No___ NA___

      c. Hearing protection   Yes___ No___ NA___

      d. Bump cap   Yes___ No___ NA___

9

Fire Extinguisher

Meets NATEF Task: Not specified by NATEF

Name _____ Date _____

Make/Model _____ Year _____ Instructor's OK [   ]

_____ 1. Describe the location of the fire extinguishers in your building or shop and note the

last inspection dates.

Type of Extinguisher	Location	Inspection Date
_____	_____	_____
_____	_____	_____
_____	_____	_____
_____	_____	_____

_____ 2. Do any of the fire extinguishers need to be charged?

_____ Yes (which ones) _____

_____ No

_____ 3. Where can the fire extinguishers be recharged? List the name and telephone number

of the company. _____ _____

_____ 4. What is the cost to recharge the fire extinguishers?

a. Water = _____

b. CO_2 = _____

c. Dry chemical = _____

10

Material Safety Data Sheet (MSDS)

Meets NATEF Task: Not specified by NATEF

Name _____ **Date** _____

Make/Model _____ **Year** _____ **Instructor's OK** [   ]

_____ **1.** Locate the MSDS sheets and describe their location _____

_____

_____ **2.** Select three commonly used chemicals or solvents. Record the following information from the MSDS:

- **Product name** _____

        chemical name(s) _____

        Does the chemical contain "chlor" or "fluor" which may indicate hazardous

        materials? **Yes** _____ **No** _____

        flash point = _____ (hopefully above 140° F)

        pH _____ (7 = neutral, higher than 7 = caustic (base), lower than 7 = acid)

- **Product name** _____

        chemical name(s) _____

        Does the chemical contain "chlor" or "fluor" which may indicate hazardous

        materials? **Yes** _____ **No** _____

        flash point = _____ (hopefully above 140° F)

        pH _____ (7 = neutral, higher than 7 = caustic (base), lower than 7 = acid)

- **Product name** _____

        chemical name(s) _____

        Does the chemical contain "chlor" or "fluor" which may indicate hazardous

        materials? **Yes** _____ **No** _____

        flash point = _____ (hopefully above 140° F)

    pH _____ **(7 = neutral, higher than 7 = caustic (base), lower than 7 = acid)**

11

Thread Repair

Meets NATEF Task: (A1-A-6) Perform thread repair (P-2, P-1)

Name _____ Date _____

Make/Model _____ Year _____ Instructor's OK [ ]

_____ **1.** Drill a hole in a piece of metal about ¼ inch thick and then thread it using a tap.

Install a bolt into the thread hole and either break it off or cut the bolt flush with the

surface.

Instructor OK _____

_____ **2.** Remove the broken off bolt using an easy out or other tool.

Instructor OK _____

_____ **3.** Using an old engine block, drill out one threaded hole in the block and install a

threaded insert, following the instructions that came with the thread insert kit.

Instructor OK _____

12

Hand Tool Identification

Meets NATEF Task: Not specified by NATEF

Name _____ Date _____

Make/Model _____ Year _____ Instructor's OK [ ]

_____ 1. List the sizes of **wrenches** you have in
your tool box. _____

_____

_____

What sizes are missing or will need to be

purchased? _____

_____

_____ 2. List the sizes of the **1/4 inch drive sockets** you have in your tool box. _____

_____

What sizes are missing or will need to be purchased? _____

_____

_____ 3. List the sizes of the **3/8 inch drive sockets** you have in your tool box. _____

_____

What sizes are missing or will need to be purchased? _____

_____

_____ 4. List the sizes of the **1/2 inch drive sockets** you have in your tool box. _____

_____

What sizes are missing or will need to be purchased? _____

_____

_____ 5. List the **other tools** you have in your tool box including hammers, screwdrivers,

pliers, and other items. _____

_____

List additional tools that you wish to add to your tool box. _____

_____

13

Power and Shop Equipment Safety Survey

Meets NATEF Task: Not specified by NATEF

Name _____ Date _____

Make/Model _____ Year _____ Instructor's OK [ ]

_____ 1. Check the power and shop equipment in the shop, at a local shop, or dealer. Where
was this survey taken? _____

_____ 2. List all shop equipment, such as hoists, floor jacks, and cranes, and not whether they
are equipped with all needed safety devices.

Shop Equipment	Safety devices? If not, list:
_____	Yes__ No__ (describe) _____
_____	Yes__ No__ (describe) _____
_____	Yes__ No__ (describe) _____
_____	Yes__ No__ (describe) _____
_____	Yes__ No__ (describe) _____
_____	Yes__ No__ (describe) _____

_____ 3. List all power equipment, such as trouble
lights, grinders, etc. and note whether they
are equipped with all needed safety devices.

Power Equipment	Safety devices? If not, list:
_____	Yes__ No__ (describe) _____
_____	Yes__ No__ (describe) _____
_____	Yes__ No__ (describe) _____
_____	Yes__ No__ (describe) _____
_____	Yes__ No__ (describe) _____

14

Vehicle Hoisting

Meets NATEF Task: Not specified by NATEF

Name _____ Date _____

Make/Model _____ Year _____ Instructor's OK [   ]

Getting Ready to Hoist the Vehicle

_____ 1. Drive the vehicle into position to be hoisted (lifted) being certain to center the vehicle in the stall.

_____ 2. Pull the vehicle forward until the front tire rests on the tire pad (if equipped).

_____ 3. Place the gear selector into the park position (if the vehicle has an automatic transmission/transaxle) or in neutral (if the vehicle has a manual transmission/transaxle) and firmly apply the parking brake.

_____ 4. Check service information for the exact location specified to place the hoist pads.
   _____

_____ 5. Position the arms and hoist pads under the frame or pinch-weld seams of the body As specified.

Hoisting the Vehicle

_____ 6. Slowly raise the hoist until the pads just contact the vehicle. Check for proper placement.

_____ 7. If the vehicle is stable and all pads are properly positioned under the vehicle, continue hoisting the vehicle to the height needed.

NOTE: Best working conditions are at chest or elbow level.

_____ 8. Be sure the safety latches have engaged before working under the vehicle.

Lowering the Vehicle

_____ 9. To lower the vehicle, raise the hoist slightly, then release the safety latches.

_____10. Lower the vehicle using the proper operating and safety release levers.

CAUTION: Do not look away while lowering the vehicle. One side of the vehicle could become stuck or something (or someone) could get under the vehicle.

_____11. After lowering the hoist arms all the way to the floor, move the arms so that they will not be hit when the vehicle is driven out of the stall.

15

Micrometer

Meets NATEF Task: Not specified by NATEF

Name _____ Date _____

Make/Model _____ Year _____ Instructor's OK [____]

A micrometer is the most used measuring instrument in engine service and repair. The thimble rotates over the barrel on a screw that has 40 threads per inch. Every revolution of the thimble moves the spindle 0.025 inch. The thimble is graduated into 25 equally spaced lines; therefore, each line represents 0.001 inch. Measure and record the following engine components.

_____ **1.** Pushrod diameter = _____

_____ **2.** Intake valve stem diameter = _____

_____ **3.** Exhaust valve stem diameter = _____

_____ **4.** Camshaft bearing diameter = _____

_____ **5.** Piston diameter = _____

        Check the factory specifications for exact location on the piston to measure the diameter.

        Location = _____

_____ **6.** Crankshaft main bearing journal diameter = _____

_____ **7.** Crankshaft rod bearing journal diameter = _____

16

We Support NATEF

Vernier Dial Caliper

Meets NATEF Task: Not specified by NATEF

Name _____ **Date** _____

Make/Model _____ **Year** _____ **Instructor's OK** ☐

A Vernier dial caliper is usually used to measure the outside diameter or length of a component such as a piston diameter or crankshaft and camshaft bearing journal diameter. Use a vernier dial caliper to measure the following items.

_____ **1.** Pushrod diameter = _____

_____ **2.** Intake valve stem diameter = _____

_____ **3.** Exhaust valve stem diameter = _____

_____ **4.** Camshaft bearing diameter = _____

_____ **5.** Piston diameter = _____

      Check the factory specifications for exact location on the piston to measure the diameter.

      Location = _____

_____ **6.** Crankshaft main bearing journal diameter = _____

_____ **7.** Crankshaft rod bearing journal diameter = _____

17

Feeler Gauge

Meets NATEF Task: Not specified by NATEF

Name _____ Date _____

Make/Model _____ Year _____ Instructor's OK [ ]

A feeler gauge (also known as a thickness gauge) is an accurately manufactured strip of metal that is used to determine the gap or clearance between two components. Use a feeler gauge to check the following.

_____ **1.** Piston ring end gap = _____

Specification = _____ (normally 0.004 in. per inch of bore)

OK _____ **NOT OK** _____

_____ **2.** Piston ring side clearance = _____

Specification = _____ (normally 0.001 to 0.003 in.)

OK _____ **NOT OK** _____

_____ **3.** Piston-to-cylinder wall clearance = _____

Specification = _____ (normally 0.001 to 0.003 in.)

OK _____ **NOT OK** _____

_____ **4.** Connecting rod side clearance = _____

Specification = _____

OK _____ **NOT OK** _____

18

Straight-Edge

Meets NATEF Task: Not specified by NATEF

Name _____ Date _____

Make/Model _____ Year _____ Instructor's OK [ ]

A straight edge is a precision ground metal measuring gauge that is used to check the flatness of engine components when used with a feeler gauge. Use a straight edge to check the flatness of the following.

_____ **1.** Cylinder heads _____

Specification = _____

OK _____ **NOT OK** _____

_____ **2.** Cylinder block deck _____

Specification = _____

OK _____ **NOT OK** _____

_____ **3.** Straightness of the main bearing bores (saddles) _____

Specification = _____

OK _____ **NOT OK** _____

19

Dial Indicator

Meets NATEF Task: Not specified by NATEF

Name _____ Date _____

Make/Model _____ Year _____ Instructor's OK [____]

A dial indicator is a precision measuring instrument used to measure movement to within thousandths of an inch. Use a dial indicator to measure the following.

_____ **1.** Crankshaft end play = _____

       Specification = _____

       OK _____ **NOT OK** _____

_____ **2.** Crankshaft runout = _____

       Specification = _____

       OK _____ **NOT OK** _____

_____ **3.** Valve guide = _____

       Specification = _____

       OK _____ **NOT OK** _____

_____ **4.** Camshaft runout = _____

       Specification = _____

       OK _____ **NOT OK** _____

20

Telescopic Gauge

Meets NATEF Task: Not specified by NATEF

Name _____ **Date** _____

Make/Model _____ **Year** _____ **Instructor's OK** ☐

A telescopic gauge is used with a micrometer to measure the inside diameter of a hole or bore. The inside diameter of a hole can be measured by inserting a telescopic gauge into the bore and rotating the handle lock to allow the arms of the gauge to contact the inside bore of the cylinder. Tighten the handle lock and remove the gauge from the cylinder. Use a micrometer to measure the telescopic gauge. Use a telescopic gauge with a micrometer and measure the following.

_____ **1.** Camshaft bearing bore = _____

Specification = _____

OK _____ **NOT OK** _____

_____ **2.** Main bearing bore (housing bore) measurement = _____

Specification = _____

OK _____ **NOT OK** _____

_____ **3.** Cylinder bore = _____

Specification = _____

OK _____ **NOT OK** _____

_____ **4.** Connecting rod big-end bore

measurement = _____

Specification = _____

OK _____ **NOT OK** _____

_____ **5.** Connecting rod small-end bore measurement = _____

Specification = _____

OK _____ **NOT OK** _____

21

Vehicle Service History

Meets NATEF Task: (A1 through A8-A-1) Research vehicle service information, vehicle service history and TSBs. (P-1)

Name _____ Date _____

Make/Model _____ Year _____ Instructor's OK [ ]

_____ 1. Search vehicle history (check all that apply).

       _____ Computerized data base (electronic file if previous service work)

       _____ Files (hard copy of previous service work)

       _____ Customer information (verbal)

       _____ Other (describe) _____

_____ 2. What electrical-related repairs have been performed in this vehicle? _____

    _____

    _____

    _____

_____ 3. From the information obtained, has the vehicle been serviced regularly?

    _____ Yes (describe the service intervals) _____

    _____

    _____

    _____ No (why?) _____

    _____

_____ 4. Based on the service history information, is the service record helpful? Why or why not? _____

    _____

    _____

22

Technical Service Bulletins

Meets NATEF Task: (A1 through A8-A-1) Research vehicle service information, vehicle service history and TSBs. (P-1)

Name _____ Date _____

Make/Model _____ Year _____ Instructor's OK [____]

_____ **1.** Technical service bulletins can be accessed through (check all that apply):

_____ Internet site(s), specify _____

_____ Paper bulletins, specify source _____

_____ CD ROM bulletins, specify source _____

_____ Other (describe) _____

_____ **2.** List all electrical-related technical service bulletins that pertain to the vehicle/engine being serviced.

Number	Description/Correction
_____	_____
_____	_____
_____	_____
_____	_____

_____ **3.** Based on this research, is the information located helpful?

_____ Yes, why? _____

_____ No, why not? _____

23

Service Manual Usage

Meets NATEF Task: (A1-A-3) Research Vehicle and Service Information, Vehicle History and TSBs (P-1)

Name _____ **Date** _____

Make/Model _____ **Year** _____ **Instructor's OK** ☐

Look up the following service information and record the page number or document number where the information was found.

Spark plug number: _____ location found _____

Spark plug gap: _____ location found _____

Number of quarts of oil for an oil change: _____ location found _____

Viscosity of engine oil recommended: _____ location found _____

Air filter part number: _____ location found _____

Fuel filter part number: _____ location found _____

AC generator (alternator) output: _____ amps location found _____

Bore and stroke of the engine: bore _____ stroke _____ location found _____

Valve cover bolt torque specification: _____ location found _____

24

VIN Code

Meets NATEF Task: (A1 through A8-A-1) Locate and interpret vehicle identification numbers.
(P-1)

Name _____ Date _____

Make/Model _____ Year _____ Instructor's OK [   ]

VIN Number _____

- The first number or letter designates the **country of origin** = _____

1 = United States	6 = Australia	L = China	V = France
2 = Canada	8 = Argentina	R = Taiwan	W = Germany
3 = Mexico	9 = Brazil	S = England	X = Russia
4 = United States	J = Japan	T = Czechoslovakia	Y = Sweden
5 = United States	K = Korea	U = Romania	Z = Italy

- The model of the vehicle is commonly the fourth or fifth character. **Model?** _____

- The eighth character is often the engine code. (Some engines cannot be determined by the VIN number.) **Engine code:** _____

- The tenth character represents the year on all vehicles. See the following chart.

VIN Year Chart (The pattern repeats every 30 years.)   **Year?** _____

A = 1980/2010	J = 1988/2018	T = 1996/2026	4 = 2004/2034
B = 1981/2011	K = 1989/2019	V = 1997/2027	5 = 2005/2035
C = 1982/2012	L = 1990/2020	W = 1998/2028	6 = 2006/2036
D = 1983/2013	M = 1991/2021	X = 1999/2029	7 = 2007/2037
E = 1984/2014	N = 1992/2022	Y = 2000/2030	8 = 2008/2038
F = 1985/2015	P = 1993/2023	1 = 2001/2031	9 = 2009/2039
G = 1986/2016	R = 1994/2024	2 = 2002/2032	
H = 1987/2017	S = 1995/2025	3 = 2003/2033	

25

Vehicle Emission Control Information

Meets NATEF Task: (A1 through A8-A-1) Research vehicle and service information. (P-1)

Name _____ Date _____

Make/Model _____ Year _____ Instructor's OK [   ]

_____ **1.** Locate the vehicle emission control information (VECI) sticker and describe its

location: _____

> **TOYOTA** | VEHICLE EMISSION CONTROL INFORMATION
> **TOYOTA MOTOR CORPORATION**
> TEST GROUP : 7TYXV01.5HC1 | EVAP. FAMILY : 7TYXR0030A42
> SFI, A/FS, WU-TWC, HO2S, TWC | 1.5 LITER
> ENGINE TUNE-UP SPECIFICATIONS FOR ALL ALTITUDES
> VALVE CLEARANCE INTAKE   0.17-0.23 mm (0.007-0.009 in.)
> (ENGINE AT COLD) EXHAUST   0.27-0.33 mm (0.011-0.013 in.)
> NO OTHER ADJUSTMENTS NEEDED.
> THIS VEHICLE CONFORMS TO U.S. EPA REGULATIONS APPLICABLE
> TO GASOLINE-FUELED 2007 MODEL YEAR NEW TIER 2 BIN 3
> MOTOR VEHICLES AND TO CALIFORNIA REGULATIONS APPLICABLE TO
> 2007 MODEL YEAR NEW LEV-II SULEV PASSENGER CARS.
> **CATALYST**
> [OBD II CERTIFIED]
> 21160   1NZ-FXE USA&CANADA   8V

_____ **2.** List what service information is included on the sticker: _____

_____

_____

_____ **3.** List emission control devices on the vehicle: _____

_____

_____

_____ **4.** What is the U.S. Federal emission rating of the vehicle? _____

_____ **5.** What is the California emission rating of the vehicle? _____

26

Vehicle Safety Certification Label

Meets NATEF Task: (A1 through A8-A-1) Locate and interpret vehicle and major component identification numbers (P-1)

Name _____ **Date** _____

Make/Model _____ **Year** _____ **Instructor's OK** ☐

_____ **1.** Describe the location of the Vehicle Safety Certification Label (usually located on the driver's side pillar post).

_____

MFD BY GENERAL MOTORS OF CANADA LTD.

DATE	GVWR	GAWR FRT	GAWR RR
06/02	2071 KG	1115 KG	956 KG
	4565 LB	2458 LB	2107 LB

THIS VEHICLE CONFORMS TO ALL APPLICABLE U.S. FEDERAL MOTOR VEHICLE SAFETY, BUMPER, AND THEFT PREVENTION STANDARDS IN EFFECT ON THE DATE OF MANUFACTURE SHOWN ABOVE.

2G1WF52E839104270   TYPE: PASS CAR

_____ **2.** What is the month and year the vehicle was manufactured?

Month = _____

Year = _____

_____ **3.** What is the gross vehicle weight rating (GVWR)?

_____

_____ **4.** What is the gross axle weight rating (GAWR)?

_____

27

Gasoline Engine Identification

Meets NATEF Task: (A8-A-1) Locate and interpret vehicle and major component identification information. (P-1)

Name _____ **Date** _____

Make/Model _____ **Year** _____ **Instructor's OK** ☐

_____ 1. Number of cylinders = _____ Arrangement of cylinders = _____

_____ 2. Number and arrangement of camshafts = _____

_____ 3. Bore = _____ Stroke = _____ Cu. in. = _____ cc = _____ Liters = _____

_____ 4. Rated HP = _____ @ RPM _____

_____ 5. Rated torque = _____ @ RPM _____

_____ 6. Compression ratio = _____

_____ 7. Recommended octane of gasoline required = _____

_____ 8. The block is constructed of: _____ cast iron _____ aluminum

_____ 9. Cylinder head(s) is constructed of: _____ cast iron _____ aluminum

_____ 10. Intake manifold is: _____ one piece _____ two pieces (upper and lower) and is

constructed of: _____ cast iron _____ aluminum _____ composite

_____ 11. Casting numbers on the block _____ Cylinder head(s) _____

Crankshaft _____

28

General Engine Specification

Meets NATEF Task: (A1-A-1) Locate and interpret vehicle and major component identification numbers. (P-1)

Name _____ Date _____

Make/Model _____ Year _____ Instructor's OK [　　]

_____ **1.** Engine type (V-6, V-8, etc.) = _____

_____ **2.** Bore = _____

_____ **3.** Stroke = _____

_____ **4.** Compression ratio = _____

_____ **5.** Displacement: cubic inches = _____

cc = _____ liter = _____

_____ **6.** Horsepower = _____ @ _____RPM

_____ **7.** Torque = _____ @ _____RPM

_____ **8.** Firing order = _____

_____ **9.** Engine oil capacity = _____

_____ **10.** Cylinder block material = _____

_____ **11.** Crankshaft material (forged steel, cast iron) = _____

_____ **12.** Cylinder head material = _____

_____ **13.** Connecting rod material (forged steel, powdered metal, etc.) = _____

COMPRESSION RATIO = 8:1   CLEARANCE VOLUME

CYLINDER VOLUME

1
2
3
4
5
6
7
8

PISTON DISPLACEMENT

BOTTOM DEAD CENTER   TOP DEAD CENTER

29

Diesel Exhaust Fluid (DEF)

Meets NATEF Task: (A8-C-5) Check and refill diesel exhaust fluid (DEF. (P-3)

Name _____ Date _____

Make/Model _____ Year _____ Instructor's OK [_____]

_____ 1. Check service information for the location of the reservoir for the diesel exhaust fluid
(DEF). Describe the location. _____

_____

_____ 2. Check service information and determine the capacity of the DEF reservoir.
_____ quarts/liters

_____ 3. Check the local area and list where DEF can be purchased.

_____

_____

_____

_____ 4. How much fluid did it take to fill the DEF reservoir? _____

30

Air Filter/Housing Inspection

Meets NATEF Task: (A8-C-2) Inspect, service or replace air filters, filter housing, and intake ducts. (P-1)

Name _____ Date _____

Make/Model _____ Year _____ Instructor's OK [ ]

_____ 1. Check service information for the specified procedure to follow to get access to the air filter. Describe specified procedure. _____

_____

_____

_____ 2. Check air filter housing for obstruction or faults. Describe the condition. _____

_____

_____

_____ 3. Describe the condition of the air filter and ducts. Check all that apply.

_____ Replaced filter with new

_____ Like new

_____ Dirty

_____ Damaged

_____ Restricted (clogged) duct

_____ Loose air filter housing/ducts

_____ Ducts and housing OK

31

Accessory Drive Belt Inspection

Meets NATEF Task: (A1-C-2) Inspect and adjust drive belts; check pulley alignment. (P-1)

Name _____ **Date** _____

Make/Model _____ **Year** _____ **Instructor's OK** ☐

     Proper operation of the alternator and the charging system as well as the water (coolant) pump and other cooling systems depend on the accessory drive belt(s).

Serpentine (poly-V) belt:

_____ **1.** Check for cracks - replace if more than 3 cracks in any one rib in 3 inches.

_____ **2.** Check for proper tension - check the tensioner notch location for proper tension position.

        OK ____ NOT OK ____

V-belts:

_____ **1.** Check belt tension:

        A. Usual specifications is 70 to 100 lb. of tension using a belt tension gauge.
        B. Maximum of ½" deflection.

        OK ____ NOT OK ____

_____ **2.** Check the belt for flaying, cracks and glazing.

        OK ____ NOT OK ____

_____ **3.** Check pulley adjustment.

        OK ____ NOT OK ____

32

High-Voltage Circuits Identification

Meets NATEF Task: (A8-B-7) Identify high-voltage circuits of electric or hybrid electric vehicles and related safety precautions. (P-3)

Name _____ Date _____

Make/Model _____ Year _____ Instructor's OK [＿＿＿]

_____ 1. Check service information for the specific precautions and identification methods used on the electric or hybrid electric vehicle being serviced. Describe the specified precautions. _____

_____

_____

_____ 2. Check all that apply.

_____ Orange cables

_____ High-voltage caution label (describe the location) _____

_____

_____ Fuse removal if being serviced (specify) _____

_____

_____ High-voltage disconnect – describe the location and procedure. _____

_____

_____ Other (describe) _____

_____

33

Engine Oil Change

Meets NATEF Task: (A1-C-5, A8-F-6) Perform oil and filter change. (P-1s)

Name _____ **Date** _____

Make/Model _____ **Year** _____ **Instructor's OK** [   ]

_____ 1. Check the owner's manual, service manual, or technical literature to determine the correct viscosity rating and quantity of oil needed.
     a. Recommended viscosity: SAE _____ or SAE _____
     b. Number of quarts (liters): with the filter _____ without the filter _____
     c. American Petroleum Institute rating (if specified) _____

_____ 2. Filter brand and number: Brand _____ Number _____

_____ 3. Hoist the vehicle safely. Position the oil drain unit under the drain plug and raise to a height about 1 foot under the drain plug.

_____ 4. Select the proper size wrench and remove the drain plug and allow the oil to drain into the drain pan.
     HINT: Apply a light force against the drain plug as you rotate it out of the oil pan. Then pull the drain plug away after unthreading the plug all the way. This helps prevent getting oil all over you and the floor!

_____ 5. After all the oil has been drained, install a new sealing washer (if needed) and install the drain plug.

_____ 6. Move the oil drain unit under the filter and remove the old oil filter.

_____ 7. Use a shop cloth and clean the oil filter gasket contact area on the engine block.

_____ 8. Apply a thin coating of engine oil to the rubber gasket on the new oil filter.

_____ 9. Install the new oil filter and hand tighten about 3/4 turn after the gasket contacts the engine block.

_____ 10. Lower the vehicle. Install the recommended quantity of engine oil using a funnel to prevent spilling oil. Replace the oil filler cap.

_____ 11. Start the engine and allow it to idle. The "oil" light should go out within 15 seconds.

_____ 12. Look under the vehicle and check for leaks at the drain plug and the oil filter.

_____ 13. Check the level of the oil again and add as necessary. **Caution:** Do not overfill!

34

Exhaust System Inspection

Meets NATEF Task: (A8-C-3 and A8-C-4) Inspect exhaust manifold, mufflers, catalytic converter(s), heat shields, and hangers; determine necessary action. (P-1)

Name _____ Date _____

Make/Model _____ Year _____ Instructor's OK [ ]

_____ 1. Check service information for the specified procedure to follow when inspecting the exhaust system. Describe the recommended procedures. _____

_____

_____ 2. Check all that apply regarding methods used to inspect the exhaust system.

       _____ Visual inspection

       _____ Tap with plastic/rubber mallet

       _____ Tester for exhaust leaks

       _____ Hangers

       _____ Heat shields

       _____ Evidence of rubbing

       _____ Broken components

       _____ Excessive rust

_____ Other (describe) _____

_____

_____ 3. Based on the inspection, what is the necessary action? _____

_____

_____

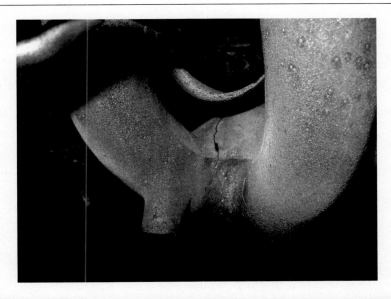

35

Cooling System Pressure Test

Meets NATEF Task: (A8-A-15, A1-C-1) Perform cooling system pressure tests; inspect and test radiator, pressure cap, coolant recovery tank, and hoses; perform necessary action. (P-1)

Name _____ Date _____

Make/Model _____ Year _____ Instructor's OK [ ]

_____ **1.** Check service information for the specified cooling system tests and specifications.

_____

_____ **2.** Pressure test the cooling system using a hand-operated pressure tester as per the tester manufacturer's instructions. Results:

_____ **OK** – pressure held
_____ **NOT OK** – pressure dropped
Describe the fault found: _____

PRESSURE
TESTER

ADAPTER

CAP

_____ **3.** Pressure test the pressure cap using a hand-operated pressure tester.

_____ **OK** – pressure held   _____ **NOT OK**

_____ **4.** Check the coolant recovery tank and hoses.

_____ **OK** – pressure held   _____ **NOT OK**

Describe fault(s) _____

_____ **5.** Check radiator for leaks or faults.

_____ **OK** – pressure held   _____ **NOT OK**

Describe fault(s) _____

_____ **6.** Based on the cooling system tests, what is the necessary action? _____

36

Test and Replace Coolant

Meets NATEF Task: (A1-C-4) Test coolant; drain and recover coolant; flush and refill cooling system with recommended coolant; bleed air as required. (P-1)

Name _____ **Date** _____

Make/Model _____ **Year** _____ **Instructor's OK** ☐

_____ **1.** Check service information for the recommended coolant testing, recover, flushing, and refilling procedures.

_____

_____

_____

_____ **2.** Drain and dispose of coolant according to federal, state and local laws.

_____ **3.** Flush and refill the coolant.

_____ **4.** What is the recommended coolant? _____

_____ **5.** Is the cooling system equipped with bleeder valves to help with bleeding trapped air from the cooling system when it is refilled?

_____ **No** _____ **Yes** (describe location) _____

_____

37

Remove and Replace Thermostat

Meets NATEF Task: (A1-C-3, A8-F-3) Inspect, test, remove and replace thermostat and gasket/seal. (P-1s)

Name _____ Date _____

Make/Model _____ Year _____ Instructor's OK [　　]

_____ 1. Check service information and determine the recommended thermostat testing and replacement procedures.

_____

_____

> **CAUTION:** Do not remove the pressure cap until the engine has cooled. The sudden drop in pressure that occurs when the cap is removed can cause the coolant to boil and cause serious burns from the escaping hot coolant.

_____ 2. Drain the cooling system into a suitable container, down to below the level of the thermostat.

_____ 3. Remove the thermostat housing bolts and housing.

_____ 4. What other components had to be removed to gain access to the thermostat housing?

_____   _____

_____   _____

_____ 5. Remove the thermostat and discard the gasket. Clean both gasket-sealing surfaces.

_____ 6. Install the replacement thermostat into the recesses in the housing bore.

_____ 7. Install a new gasket and reinstall the thermostat housing and retaining bolts.

_____ 8. Torque the thermostat housing to factory specification.

Thermostat housing bolt torque specification = _____

_____ 9. Refill the cooling system with new coolant.

> **CAUTION:** Be sure to open the cooling system bleeder valves(s), if equipped, to avoid trapping air.

_____ 10. Install the radiator pressure cap and start the engine. Check for leaks and proper cooling system operation.

38

Fluids Check

Meets NATEF Task: (A1-A-3) Inspect engine for fuel, oil, coolant and other leaks; determine necessary action. (P-2)

Name _____ **Date** _____

Make/Model _____ **Year** _____ **Instructor's OK** ☐

_____ 1. Check service information for the recommended procedures to follow to locate engine

fluid leaks (describe). _____

_____

_____ 2. Check the engine oil level and condition.

        Level: _____low _____okay _____overfilled

        Color: _____black _____dark brown _____amber

_____ 3. Check the radiator coolant level (check when cold only!). The coolant should be

within 3" of the top of the filler neck. (The reserve tank should be filled to the

indicated mark with a 50/50 mixture of antifreeze and water.)

_____ 4. Based on the inspection, what is the necessary action? _____

_____

_____

39

Fluid Leakage Diagnosis

Meets NATEF Task: (A1-A-3) Inspect engine assembly for fuel, coolant, and other leaks; determine necessary action. (P-1)

___

Name _____ Date _____

Make/Model _____ Year _____ Instructor's OK [ ]

Fluid colors include the following:

- **red** – automatic transmission fluid (also could be in some cooling systems)
- **green** – antifreeze coolant
- **orange** – antifreeze coolant
- **blue** – antifreeze coolant or windshield washer fluid
- **yellow** – windshield washer fluid
- **clear** – condensation from the air-conditioning system (normal)

_____ **1.** Safely hoist the vehicle and carefully inspect the underneath of the vehicle.

_____ **2.** Where is the highest, most forward area of the leak? (describe) _____

_____

_____ **3.** If the exact location cannot be located, lower the vehicle and add fluorescent dye to the unit believed to be leaking oil. Drive the vehicle for 10 to 15 minutes and hoist the vehicle.

_____ **4.** Using black light, locate the area of the leak by looking for the yellow/green areas highlighted by the dye. Describe the leak location: _____

_____

_____ **5.** Based on the inspection for oil leaks, what is the

necessary action? _____

_____

40

Oil Leak Diagnosis

Meets NATEF Task: (A1-A-3) Inspect engine assembly for fuel, oil, coolant, and other leaks; determine necessary action. (P-1)

Name _____ Date _____

Make/Model _____ Year _____ Instructor's OK [   ]

Engine oil is usually amber in color when new, but quickly becomes darker and often black when used in an engine.

_____ **1.** Raise the hood and carefully inspect the areas where oil is likely to leak including:

        valve covers   – **OK** _____   **NOT OK** _____

        intake manifold area   – **OK** _____   **NOT OK** _____

        oil pressure-sending unit   – **OK** _____   **NOT OK** _____

_____ **2.** Safely hoist the vehicle and carefully inspect the underneath of the engine.

_____ **3.** Where is the highest, most forward area of the leak? (describe) _____

_____

_____ **4.** If the exact location cannot be located, lower the vehicle and add fluorescent dye to the engine oil. Drive the vehicle for 10 to 15 minutes and hoist the vehicle.

_____ **5.** Using black light, locate the area of the leak by looking for the yellow/green areas highlighted by the dye. Describe the leak location: _____

_____

_____ **6.** Based on the test results, what is the necessary action? _____

_____

41

Oil Pressure Measurement

Meets NATEF Task: (A1-A-2) Verify operation of the instrument panel engine warning indicators (P-1)

Name _____ Date _____

Make/Model _____ Year _____ Instructor's OK [　　]

_____ **1.** Locate the oil pressure-sending (sender) unit.

_____ **2.** Remove the sending unit using the proper size sending unit socket or wrench.

_____ **3.** Thread a mechanical oil pressure gauge into the thread portion of the engine block where the sending unit was located.

_____ **4.** Route the oil pressure gauge hose away from the moving components of the engine.

_____ **5.** Start the engine and check for leaks.

_____ **6.** Record the oil pressure:

    oil pressure @ idle _____

    oil pressure @ 1,000 RPM _____

    oil pressure @ 2,000 RPM _____

    oil pressure @ 3,000 RPM _____

    NOTE: Most engines require about 10 psi per 1,000 RPM.

_____ **7.** Based on the test results, what is the necessary action? _____

    _____

42

Paper Test

Meets NATEF Task: (A8-A-3) Diagnose engine mechanical concerns; determine necessary action. (P-1)

Name _____ Date _____

Make/Model _____ Year _____ Instructor's OK [ ]

_____ **1.** The engine should be at normal operating temperature (the upper radiator hose hot and pressurized).

_____ **2.** Start the engine and allow it to idle. A sound running engine should produce even and steady exhaust at the tailpipe.

_____ **3.** Hold a piece of paper (even a dollar bill works) or a 3" x 5" card within 1 inch (25 mm) of the tailpipe with the engine running at idle. The paper should blow out evenly without "puffing".

    a. If the paper is drawn toward the tailpipe at times, the valves in one or more cylinders could be burned. Other possible problems if the paper is sucked toward the tailpipe include:

        1. The engine could be misfiring due to a lean condition that could occur normally when the engine is cold.

        2. Pulsing of the paper toward the tailpipe could also be caused by a hole in the exhaust system. If exhaust escapes through a hole in the exhaust system, air could be drawn from the tailpipe to the hole in the exhaust between the exhaust "puffs," causing the paper to be drawn toward the tailpipe.

    b. If the paper is unevenly pulsing outward, an engine misfire is a possibility. The usual cause of this is an ignition or an engine mechanical problem such as a worn camshaft or broken rocker arm.

_____ **4.** Based on the test results, what is the necessary action? _____

_____

43

Vacuum Testing

Meets NATEF Task: (A8-A-2) Perform engine absolute (vacuum/boost) manifold pressure tests; determine necessary action. (P-1)

Name _____ Date _____

Make/Model _____ Year _____ Instructor's OK [   ]

_____ 1. Connect the vacuum gauge to a manifold vacuum source.

_____ 2. Vacuum at idle = _____ in. Hg. (should be 17-21 in. Hg. and steady).

_____ 3. Snap accelerate the engine. (Vacuum should drop close to zero, and then increase higher than the idle vacuum snap reading.

_____ / _____

_____ 4. Drive the vehicle on a level road in high gear at a steady speed.

Cruise vacuum = _____ in. Hg. (should be 10 - 15 in. Hg.)

_____ 5. Accelerate the vehicle in high gear to W.O.T.

W.O.T. vacuum = _____ in. Hg. (should be almost zero)

_____ 6. Decelerate the vehicle from 50 MPH with the throttle closed.

Deceleration vacuum = _____ in. Hg. (should be higher than idle vacuum)

_____ 7. With the engine out of gear and the brake firmly applied, raise the engine speed to 2,000 RPM and hold for one full minute. This tests for an exhaust restriction.

Results = _____ in. Hg.

_____ 8. Stop the engine. Disable the ignition or the fuel ignition system. Crank the engine and observe the vacuum during cranking.

Cranking vacuum = _____ in. Hg. (should be higher than 2.5 in. Hg.)

_____ 9. Based on the test results, what is the necessary action? _____

_____

44

Power Balance – Manual Method

Meets NATEF Task: (A8-A-3) Perform cylinder balance test; determine necessary action.
(P-2)

Name _____ Date _____

Make/Model _____ Year _____ Instructor's OK [   ]

_____ 1. Check service information for the recommended method and procedures to follow for performing a power balance test without the use of a scan tool.

_____ 2. One method uses a 2" long vacuum hose between the distributor cap (or coils) and the spark plug wires.

_____ 3. Connect the tachometer to the engine and record idle RPM = _____.

_____ 4. Using a test light, ground out one cylinder at a time by touching the tip of the grounded test light to the section of rubber hose, and record the RPM drop:

#1 _____   #5 _____

#2 _____   #6 _____

#3 _____   #7 _____

#4 _____   #8 _____

NOTE: 50 RPM is the maximum variation between cylinders. The cylinder that drops the most RPM is the *strongest* cylinder. The cylinder that drops RPM the least is the *weakest* cylinder.

_____ 5. Results:

RPM difference between the strongest and weakest cylinder _____.

Which cylinder is the strongest? _____.

Which cylinder is the weakest? _____.

_____ 6. Based on the test results, what is the necessary action? _____

_____

45

Power Balance – Scan Tool Method

Meets NATEF Task: (A8-A-3) Perform cylinder balance test; determine necessary action.
(P-2)

Name _____ Date _____

Make/Model _____ Year _____ Instructor's OK [＿＿]

_____ 1. Check service information for the specified procedures to follow to perform a power balance test using a scan tool.

_____ 2. Connect a scan tool to the data link connector (DLC) and select power balance on the injector balance test.

_____ 3. Following the instructions on the scan tool, perform a power balance test.

_____ 4. Record the RPM drop:

#1 _____   #5 _____

#2 _____   #6 _____

#3 _____   #7 _____

#4 _____   #8 _____

NOTE: 50 RPM is the maximum variation between cylinders. The cylinder that drops the most RPM is the *strongest* cylinder. The cylinder that drops RPM the least is the *weakest* cylinder.

_____ 5. Results:

RPM difference between the strongest and weakest cylinder _____.

Which cylinder is the strongest? _____.

Which cylinder is the weakest? _____.

_____ 6. Based on the test results, what is the necessary action? _____

_____

46

Compression Testing

Meets NATEF Task: (A8-A-4) Perform cylinder cranking and running compression tests; determine necessary action. (P-1)

Name _____ Date _____

Make/Model _____ Year _____ Instructor's OK ☐

_____ **1.** Remove all spark plugs (be certain to label the spark plug wires).

_____ **2.** Block open the throttle and choke (if equipped).

_____ **3.** Perform compression testing during cranking (4 "puffs").

> **NOTE:** For accurate test results, the engine should be at normal operating temperature. The 1st puff should be at least 50% of the final puff. (A low 1st puff reading indicates possible weak piston rings.)

RESULTS: **1st puff/final reading**   **1st puff/final reading**

1. _____/_____   5. _____/_____
2. _____/_____   6. _____/_____
3. _____/_____   7. _____/_____
4. _____/_____   8. _____/_____

_____ **4.** Perform a **wet compression test** on any cylinder that reads lower-than-normal on the cranking compression test. Add about 1 ounce of engine oil to the cylinder and repeat the test.

	Cranking Compression Reading	**Wet Compression Reading**
Cylinder #1	_____	_____
Cylinder #2	_____	_____
Cylinder #3	_____	_____
Cylinder #4	_____	_____
Cylinder #5	_____	_____
Cylinder #6	_____	_____
Cylinder #7	_____	_____
Cylinder #8	_____	_____

If the wet compression reading is a lot higher than the cranking compression reading, the piston rings are worn.

_____ **5.** Based on the test results, what is the necessary action? _____

47

Running Compression Test

Meets NATEF Task: (A8-A-4) Perform cylinder and running compression tests; determine necessary action. (P-1)

Name _____ **Date** _____

Make/Model _____ **Year** _____ **Instructor's OK** [ ]

_____ 1. Perform a normal cranking compression test to eliminate obvious engine mechanical faults.

_____ 2. Install the spark plugs except for one. Use a jumper wire on the one remaining spark plug wire and connect the spark plug wire to ground to prevent damage to the coil or the ignition control module.

_____ 3. Install the compression gauge, start the engine, and operate at idle speed (push on the Schrader valve and release the pressure every 5 or 6 "puffs").

_____ 4. Snap open the accelerator and note the gauge reading. It should increase.

_____ 5. Record all cylinders for running (idle) and snap accelerator readings.

> Cylinder #1 Idle _____ Snap _____ Cylinder #5 Idle _____ Snap _____
> Cylinder #2 Idle _____ Snap _____ Cylinder #6 Idle _____ Snap _____
> Cylinder #3 Idle _____ Snap _____ Cylinder #7 Idle _____ Snap _____
> Cylinder #4 Idle _____ Snap _____ Cylinder #8 Idle _____ Snap _____

_____ 6. Analysis:

> Running compression at idle speed should be about half of the cranking compression test (60 to 80 psi). ____ **OK** ____ **NOT OK**

> Snap throttle compression should be about 80% of the cranking compression (100 to 130 psi).

> - All cylinders should be within 10% of each other on both tests.
> - If the snap throttle or idle reading is low, look for a restricted intake, worn cam lobe, bent pushrod, or defective rocker arm.
> - If the snap throttle reading is higher than 80% of the cranking compression test, look for a restricted exhaust on that cylinder, such as a worn exhaust cam lobe or a collapsed lifter. If all cylinders are high on the snap throttle test, look for a restricted catalytic converter or other restriction.

_____ 7. Based on the test results, what is the necessary action? _____

48

Relative Compression

Meets NATEF Task: (A8-A-4) Perform cylinder and running compression tests; determine necessary action. (P-1)

Name _____ Date _____

Make/Model _____ Year _____ Instructor's OK [ ]

Many scopes, such as the Fluke 98 scopemeter and MTS 5100, are capable of displaying changes in battery voltage when the engine is being cranked and display a relative compression based on the voltage change. For example, if a particular cylinder is weak and lacks compression, the starter motor will not have to draw as much current from the battery whenever that cylinder is being rotated through its compression stroke. The lower compression is reflected by a higher than normal battery voltage and displayed on the display as a lower than normal reading.

_____ 1. Connect the scope to the battery positive (+) and negative (–) terminals. Connect a probe to cylinder #1 needed to "sync" the display to cylinder #1. (Check and follow the scope manufacturer's recommended procedure.)

_____ 2. Disable the ignition to prevent the engine from starting while it is being cranked.

> **NOTE:** The ignition system must be disabled or grounded to prevent possible ignition coil damage that could result.

_____ 3. Crank the engine for 15 seconds and observe the scope pattern. If all cylinders are almost equal condition, the display should also be equal. If unequal test results are indicated, the engine should be tested further by performing a compression test and a cylinder leakage test.

_____ 4. Based on the test results, what is the necessary action?

_____

_____

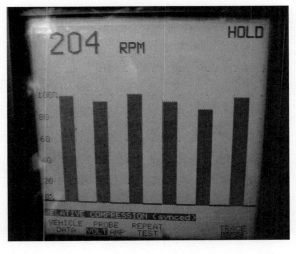

49

Cylinder Leakage Test

Meets NATEF Task: (A8-A-5) Perform cylinder leakage test; determine necessary action.
(P-1)

Name _____ Date _____

Make/Model _____ Year _____ Instructor's OK [ ]

_____ **1.** The engine should be at normal operating temperature.

_____ **2.** Test the cylinder with the piston at top dead center (TDC) on the compression stroke.

_____ **3.** Calibrate the tester and install tester lead in the spark plug opening.

_____ **4.** Install compressed air in the cylinder. Read the meter.

Cylinder #1 _____ % of leakage
Cylinder #2 _____ % of leakage
Cylinder #3 _____ % of leakage
Cylinder #4 _____ % of leakage
Cylinder #5 _____ % of leakage
Cylinder #6 _____ % of leakage
Cylinder #7 _____ % of leakage
Cylinder #8 _____ % of leakage

Results:

Good   - less than 10%

Acceptable   - less than 20%

Unacceptable - higher than 20%

_____ **5.** Check the *source* of air leakage:

_____ A. radiator - possible blown head gasket or cracked cylinder head.

_____ B. tail pipe - defective exhaust valve(s).

_____ C. carburetor or air inlet - defective intake valve(s).

_____ D. oil fill cap - possible worn or defective piston rings.

_____ **6.** Based on the test results, what is the necessary action? _____

_____

50

Verify Engine Operating Temperature

Meets NATEF Task: (A8-A-6) Verify engine operating temperature; determine necessary action. (P-1)

Name _____ Date _____

Make/Model _____ Year _____ Instructor's OK [ ]

_____ 1. Check service information for specified engine operating temperature, which is generally between the thermostat temperature rating and 20°F above the thermostat temperature.

      Thermostat temperature = _____
      Normal coolant temperature range = _____

Thermostat Temperature	Normal Operating Temperature
180°F (82°C)	Between 180° and 200°F (82° and 93°C)
195°F (91°C)	Between 195° and 215°F (91° and 102°C)

_____ 2. Determine the operating temperature of the engine by as many methods as possible including:

- Dash temperature gauge = _____
- Scan tool (ECT) = _____
- Infrared pyrometer = _____
- Other (specify) _____

_____ 3. Based on the result of the engine operating temperature measurements, what is the necessary action?

_____

_____

51

Remove and Replace Timing Belt

Meets NATEF Task: (A1-B-1, A8-F-2) Remove and replace timing belt; verify correct camshaft timing. (P-1)

Name _____ Date _____

Make/Model _____ Year _____ Instructor's OK [ ]

_____ 1. Check service information for the exact timing belt replacement procedure as specified by the vehicle manufacturer, including torque specifications.

_____

_____

_____

_____ 2. Inspect the timing belt for wear or faults.

_____ 3. List the parts recommended to be replaced when replacing the timing belt. (Usually includes the water pump, camshaft seals, crankshaft seals, and often the tensioner[s].)

SURFACE CRACK   WORN EDGE

SIDEWALL CRACK   PLY SEPARATION

_____

_____

_____ 4. Describe the proper camshaft timing procedure. _____

_____

_____ 5. What parts were inspected for wear? _____

_____

_____ 6. What parts were replaced? _____

_____

_____ 7. Verify the correct camshaft timing. _____

_____

52

Valve Adjustment

Meets NATEF Task: (A8-F-1) Adjust valves on engines with mechanical or hydraulic lifters.
(P-1)

Name _____ Date _____

Make/Model _____ Year _____ Instructor's OK [ ]

_____ 1. Check service information and determine the specified procedure to follow to adjust
the valves. List the procedure:

_____

_____

SPECIAL TOOL   ADJUSTING DISC   MAGNET

_____ 2. Compare the original valve clearance or adjustment to the specified clearance.

		Original	Specified
Cylinder #1	Intake	_____	_____
	Exhaust	_____	_____
Cylinder #2	Intake	_____	_____
	Exhaust	_____	_____
Cylinder #3	Intake	_____	_____
	Exhaust	_____	_____
Cylinder #4	Intake	_____	_____
	Exhaust	_____	_____
Cylinder #5	Intake	_____	_____
	Exhaust	_____	_____
Cylinder #6	Intake	_____	_____
	Exhaust	_____	_____
Cylinder #7	Intake	_____	_____
	Exhaust	_____	_____
Cylinder #8	Intake	_____	_____
	Exhaust	_____	_____

53

Hybrid Engine Service Precautions

Meets NATEF Task: (A1-A-7, A8-F-7) Identify hybrid vehicle internal combustion engine service precautions. (P-3)

Name _____ **Date** _____

Make/Model _____ **Year** _____ **Instructor's OK** ⬚

_____ 1. Check service information for the internal combustion engine (ICE) service precautions for the hybrid electric vehicle being serviced. List specified precautions.

  _____

  _____

  _____

  _____

  _____

  _____

_____ 2. The safety procedures include (check all that apply):

  _____ "Ready" light off before servicing

  _____ High voltage disconnected before servicing

  _____ Setup cones around the vehicle before servicing

  _____ Other (describe) _____

_____ 3. List all service to the engine that is different from a typical non-hybrid engine including such items as oil viscosity (SAE rating) and spark plugs.

  _____

  _____

  _____

54

Cover Gasket Replacement

Meets NATEF Task: (A1-A-4) Install engine covers, using gaskets and seals as required.
(P-1)

Name _____ Date _____

Make/Model _____ Year _____ Instructor's OK [   ]

_____ **1.** Check service information for the procedure to follow when replacing the valve cover
gaskets. _____
_____
_____

_____ **2.** List the parts and components that have to be removed to gain access to the valve
covers.

_____   _____   _____   _____
_____   _____   _____   _____

_____ **3.** Type of gasket used?

_____ RTV   _____ cork   _____ cork/rubber   _____ rubber
_____ other (specify) _____

_____ **4.** Clean both gasket surfaces thoroughly.

_____ **5.** Install a new gasket. What type of replacement gasket is being used?

_____ RTV   _____ cork   _____ cork/rubber   _____ rubber
_____ other (specify) _____

_____ **6.** Torque the valve cover retaining bolts to factory specifications.

Valve cover bolt tightening torque specification = _____

_____ **7.** Complete the repair by reassembling the components previously removed.

_____ **8.** Start the engine and check for proper engine operation and look for oil leaks from the
valve cover.

OK _____   **NOT OK** _____

Describe the problem: _____

_____

55

Electrical Fundamentals

Meets NATEF Task: Not specified by NATEF

Name _____ Date _____

Make/Model _____ Year _____ Instructor's OK ☐

_____ **1.** State the relationship among volts, amperes, and ohms.

_____

_____

_____

_____ **2.** List five sources of electricity.

     a. _____

     b. _____

     c. _____

     d. _____

     e. _____

_____ **3.** Describe what occurs to resistance when:

     a. The conductor length is increased _____

     b. The conductor diameter is increased _____

     c. The temperature of the conductor is increased _____

_____ **4.** What is the difference between a rheostat and a potentiometer? _____

_____

_____

56

Electrical Circuit Problems

Meets NATEF Task: (A6-A-5) Demonstrate knowledge of the causes and effects of shorts, grounds, opens, and high resistance. (P-1)

Name _____ Date _____

Make/Model _____ Year _____ Instructor's OK [   ]

_____ 1. What is the effect on an electrical circuit due to a short? _____

_____

_____

_____ 2. What is the effect on an electrical circuit due to an unintentional ground? _____

_____

_____

_____ 3. What is the effect on an electrical circuit due to an open? _____

_____

_____

_____ 4. What is the effect on an electrical circuit due to high resistance? _____

_____

_____

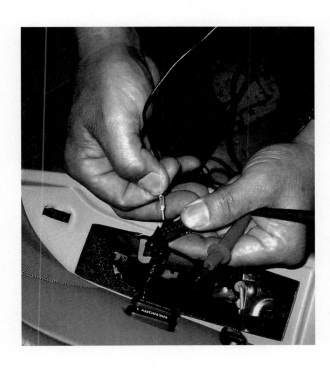

57

Identify/Interpret Electrical Systems Concerns

Meets NATEF Task: (A6-A-2) Identify and interpret electrical/electronic concerns; determine necessary action. (P-1)

Name _____ Date _____

Make/Model _____ Year _____ Instructor's OK ☐

_____ **1.** Describe electrical/electronic concerns. _____

_____

_____ **2.** Can the concern be verified? _____ **Yes** _____ **No**

If no, ask the customer for additional information. _____

_____

_____ **3.** Are there any stored diagnostic trouble codes (DTCs)?

_____ **Yes** (describe) _____

_____ **No**

_____ **4.** Perform a thorough visual inspection of the
related components and wiring.

_____ **OK**

_____ **NOT OK** (describe) _____

_____ **5.** Check service information for steps and procedures to
determine and correct the fault.

_____

_____

_____ **6.** Based on the above inspection and research, what is the necessary action?

_____

_____

58

Name _____ Date _____

Series Circuit Worksheet #1

Meets NATEF Task: (A6-A-2) Diagnose electrical/electronic integrity for series, parallel, and series-parallel circuits using principles of electricity. (Ohm's Law).

1.

E = 12 volts
I_T = 3 amperes
R_T = _____

2.

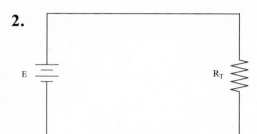

E = 12 volts
I_T = _____
R_T = 3 ohms

3.

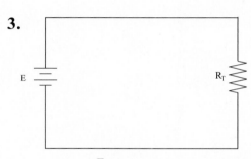

E = _____
I_T = 3 amperes
R_T = 4 ohms

4.

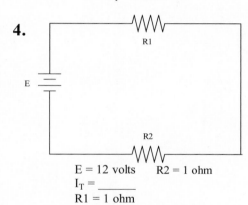

E = 12 volts   R2 = 1 ohm
I_T = _____
R1 = 1 ohm

5.

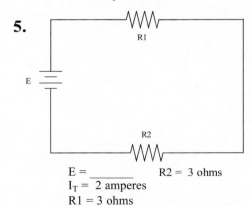

E = _____   R2 = 3 ohms
I_T = 2 amperes
R1 = 3 ohms

6.

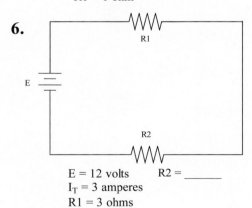

E = 12 volts   R2 = _____
I_T = 3 amperes
R1 = 3 ohms

59

Name _____ Date _____

Series Circuit Worksheet #2

Meets NATEF Task: (A6-A-2) Diagnose electrical/electronic integrity for series, parallel, and series-parallel circuits using principles of electricity. (Ohm's Law).

1.

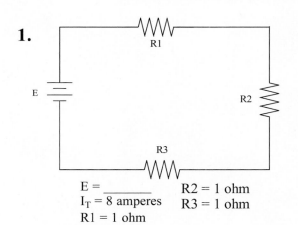

E = _____   R2 = 1 ohm
I_T = 8 amperes   R3 = 1 ohm
R1 = 1 ohm

2.

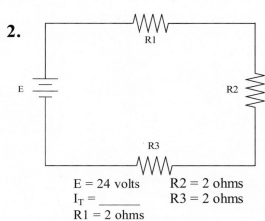

E = 24 volts   R2 = 2 ohms
I_T = _____   R3 = 2 ohms
R1 = 2 ohms

3.

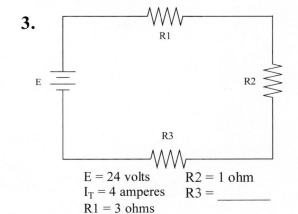

E = 24 volts   R2 = 1 ohm
I_T = 4 amperes   R3 = _____
R1 = 3 ohms

4.

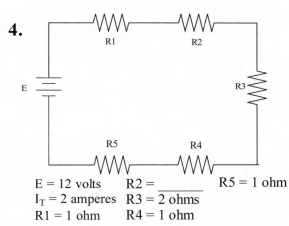

E = 12 volts   R2 = _____   R5 = 1 ohm
I_T = 2 amperes   R3 = 2 ohms
R1 = 1 ohm   R4 = 1 ohm

5.

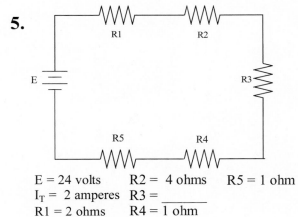

E = 24 volts   R2 = 4 ohms   R5 = 1 ohm
I_T = 2 amperes   R3 = _____
R1 = 2 ohms   R4 = 1 ohm

6.

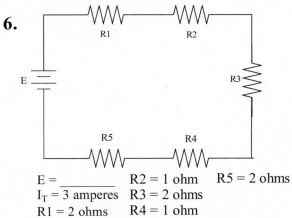

E = _____   R2 = 1 ohm   R5 = 2 ohms
I_T = 3 amperes   R3 = 2 ohms
R1 = 2 ohms   R4 = 1 ohm

60

Name _____ **Date** _____

Series Circuit Worksheet #3

Meets NATEF Task: (A6-A-2) Diagnose Electrical/Electronic Integrity for Series, Parallel, and Series-Parallel Circuits Using Principles of Electricity (Ohm's Law).

1.

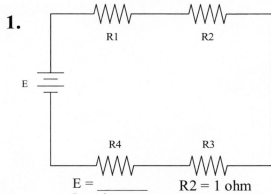

E = _____
I_T = 6 amperes
R1 = 1 ohm

R2 = 1 ohm
R3 = 1 ohm
R4 = 1 ohm

2.

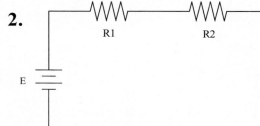

E = _____
I_T = 3 amperes
R1 = 0.5 ohms

R2 = 1 ohm
R3 = 0.5 ohms
R4 = 1 ohm

3.

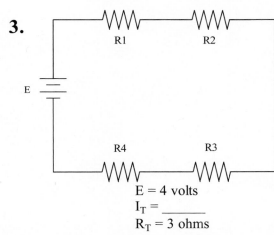

E = 4 volts
I_T = _____
R_T = 3 ohms

4.

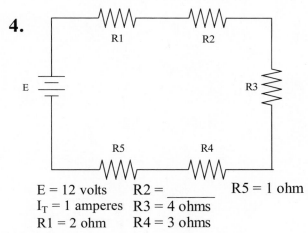

E = 12 volts
I_T = 1 amperes
R1 = 2 ohm

R2 = _____
R3 = 4 ohms
R4 = 3 ohms

R5 = 1 ohm

5.

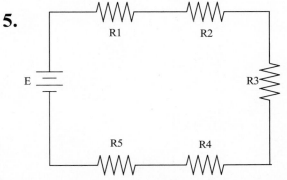

E = 24 volts
I_T = 12 amperes
R1 = 0.5 ohms

R2 = 0.5 ohms
R3 = _____
R4 = 0.5 ohms

R5 = 0.25 ohms

6.

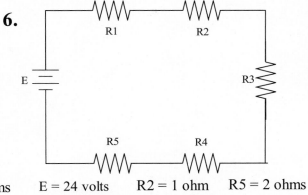

E = 24 volts
I_T = 3 amperes
R1 = 2 ohms

R2 = 1 ohm
R3 = 2 ohms
R4 = _____

R5 = 2 ohms

61

We Support
NATEF

Name _____ **Date** _____

Parallel Circuit Worksheet #1

Meets NATEF Task: (A6-A-2) Diagnose Electrical/Electronic Integrity for Series, Parallel, and Series-Parallel Circuits Using Principles of Electricity (Ohm's Law).

1.
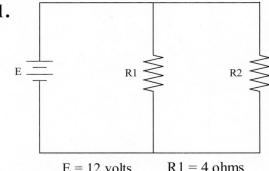

$E = 12$ volts $R1 = 4$ ohms
$I_T = $ _____ $R2 = 4$ ohms

2.
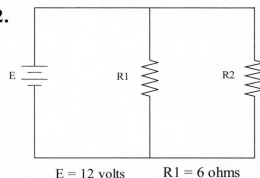

$E = 12$ volts $R1 = 6$ ohms
$I_T = 4$ amperes $R2 = $ _____

3.
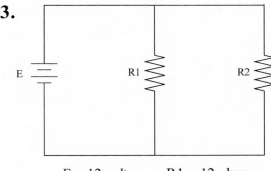

$E = 12$ volts $R1 = 12$ ohms
$I_T = $ _____ $R2 = 12$ ohms

4.
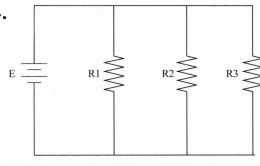

$E = 12$ volts $R2 = 4$ ohms
$I_T = $ _____ $R3 = 2$ ohms
$R1 = 4$ ohms

5.
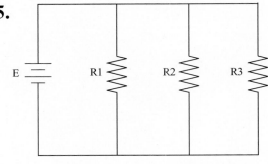

$E = $ _____ $R2 = 4$ ohms
$I_T = 12$ amperes $R3 = 4$ ohms
$R1 = 2$ ohms

6.
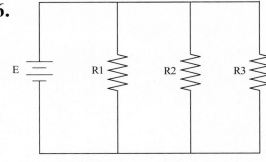

$E = 12$ volts $R2 = $ _____
$I_T = 12$ amperes $R3 = 2$ ohms
$R1 = 4$ ohms

62

Name _____ Date _____

Parallel Circuit Worksheet #2

Meets NATEF Task: (A6-A-2) Diagnose Electrical/Electronic Integrity for Series, Parallel, and Series-Parallel Circuits Using Principles of Electricity (Ohm's Law).

1.

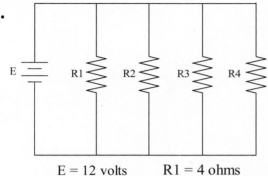

E = 12 volts   R1 = 4 ohms
I_T = _____   R2 = 12 ohms
R1 = 4 ohms   R4 = 12 ohms

2.

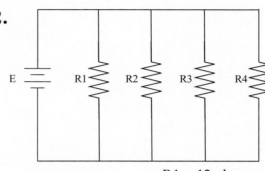

E = _____   R1 = 12 ohms
I_T = 4 amperes   R2 = 12 ohms
R1 = 12 ohms   R3 = 12 ohms

3.

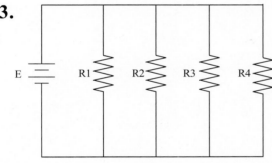

E = _____   R2 = 4 ohms
I_T = 1 ampere   R3 = 6 ohms
R1 = 2 ohms   R4 = 12 ohms

4.

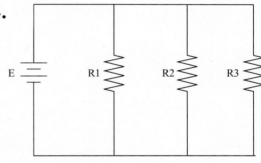

E = 12 volts   R2 = 8 ohms
I_T = _____   R3 = 4 ohms
R1 = 8 ohms

5.

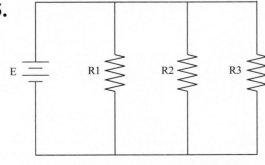

E = 12 volts   R2 = 12 ohms
I_T = 4 amperes   R3 = _____
R1 = 12 ohms

6.

E = _____   R2 = 24 ohms
I_T = 2 amperes   R3 = 12 ohms
R1 = 24 ohms

63

Name _____ Date _____

Parallel Circuit Worksheet #3

Meets NATEF Task: (A6-A-2) Diagnose Electrical/Electronic Integrity for Series, Parallel, and Series-Parallel Circuits Using Principles of Electricity (Ohm's Law).

1.

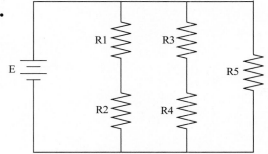

E = 12 volts   R2 = 8 ohms   R5 = 8 ohms
I_T = _____   R3 = 8 ohms
R1 = 8 ohms   R4 = 8 ohms

2.

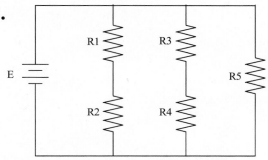

E = 24 volts   R2 = 4 ohms   R5 = 4 ohms
I_T = _____   R3 = 4 ohms
R1 = 4 ohms   R4 = 4 ohms

3.

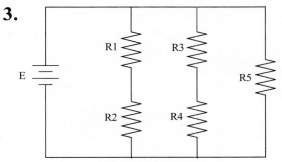

E = _____   R2 = 2 ohms   R5 = 4 ohms
I_T = 6 amperes   R3 = 2 ohms
R1 = 2 ohms   R4 = 2 ohms

4.

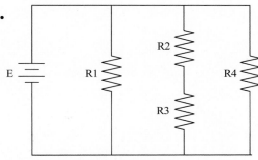

E = 12 volts   R2 = _____
I_T = 4 amperes   R3 = 4 ohms
R1 = 9 ohms   R4 = 9 ohms

5.

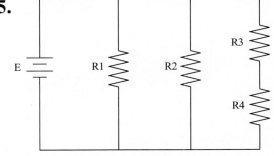

E = 24 volts   R2 = 12 ohms
I_T = 6 amperes   R3 = _____
R1 = 12 ohms   R4 = 6 ohms

6.

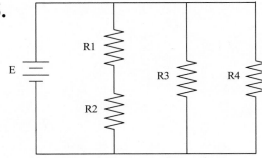

E = 12 volts   R2 = 12 ohms
I_T = 2 amperes   R3 = 18 ohms
R1 = _____   R4 = 18 ohms

Name _____ Date _____

Series-Parallel Circuit Worksheet #1

Meets NATEF Task: (A6-A-2) Diagnose Electrical/Electronic Integrity for Series, Parallel, and Series-Parallel Circuits Using Principles of Electricity (Ohm's Law).

1.

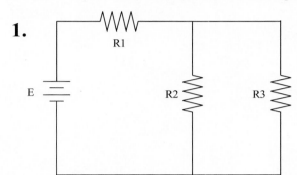

E = 12 volts   R2 = 4 ohms
I_T = 3 amperes   R3 = 4 ohms
R1 = _____

2.

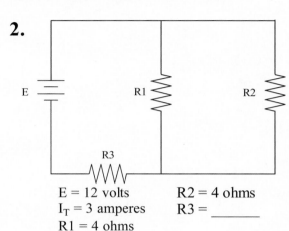

E = 12 volts   R2 = 4 ohms
I_T = 3 amperes   R3 = _____
R1 = 4 ohms

3.

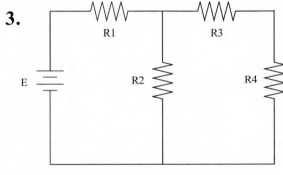

E = 12 volts   R2 = 4 ohms
I_T = _____   R3 = 2 ohms
R1 = 2 ohms   R4 = 2 ohms

4.

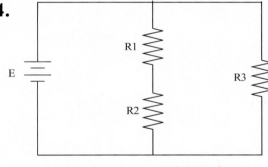

E = _____   R2 = 4 ohms
I_T = 3 amperes   R3 = 8 ohms
R1 = 4 ohms

5.

E = 12 volts   R3 = 2 ohms
I_T = _____   R4 = 4 ohms
R1 = 2 ohms   R5 = 2 ohms
R2 = 8 ohms

6.

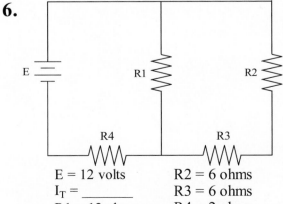

E = 12 volts   R2 = 6 ohms
I_T = _____   R3 = 6 ohms
R1 = 12 ohms   R4 = 2 ohms

65

Name _____ **Date** _____

Series-Parallel Circuit Worksheet #2

Meets NATEF Task: (A6-A-2) Diagnose Electrical/Electronic Integrity for Series, Parallel, and Series-Parallel Circuits Using Principles of Electricity (Ohm's Law).

1.

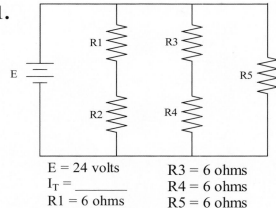

E = 24 volts   R3 = 6 ohms
I_T = _____   R4 = 6 ohms
R1 = 6 ohms   R5 = 6 ohms
R2 = 6 ohms

2.

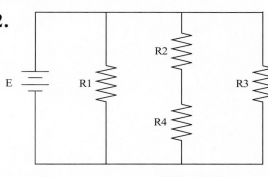

E = _____   R2 = 4 ohms
I_T = 12 amperes   R3 = 4 ohms
R1 = 8 ohms   R4 = 4 ohms

3.

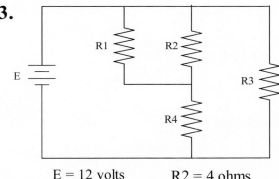

E = 12 volts   R2 = 4 ohms
I_T = _____   R3 = 4 ohms
R1 = 4 ohms   R4 = 2 ohms

4.

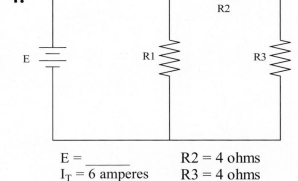

E = _____   R2 = 4 ohms
I_T = 6 amperes   R3 = 4 ohms
R1 = 8 ohms

5.

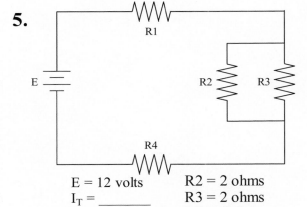

E = 12 volts   R2 = 2 ohms
I_T = _____   R3 = 2 ohms
R1 = 1 ohm   R4 = 1 ohm

6.

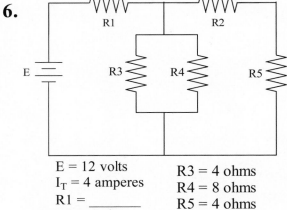

E = 12 volts   R3 = 4 ohms
I_T = 4 amperes   R4 = 8 ohms
R1 = _____   R5 = 4 ohms
R2 = 4 ohms

66

Name _____ Date _____

Series-Parallel Circuit Worksheet #3

Meets NATEF Task: (A6-A-2) Diagnose Electrical/Electronic Integrity for Series, Parallel, and Series-Parallel Circuits Using Principles of Electricity (Ohm's Law).

1.

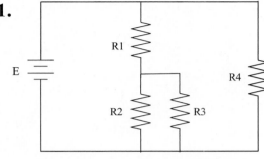

E = 12 volts   R2 = 12 ohms
I_T = 2 amperes   R3 = _____
R1 = 6 ohms   R4 = 12 ohms

2.

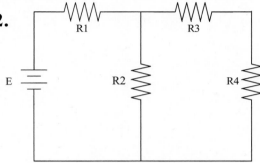

E = 24 volts   R2 = 8 ohms
I_T = _____   R3 = 4 ohms
R1 = 2 ohms   R4 = 4 ohms

3.

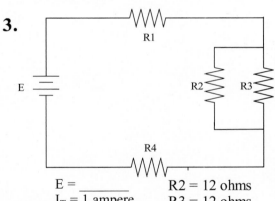

E = _____   R2 = 12 ohms
I_T = 1 ampere   R3 = 12 ohms
R1 = 2 ohms   R4 = 4 ohms

4.

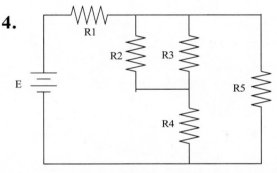

E = 24 volts   R2 = 12 ohms   R5 = 12 ohms
I_T = _____   R3 = 12 ohms
R1 = 6 ohms   R4 = 6 ohms

5.

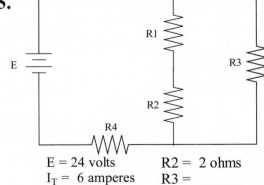

E = 24 volts   R2 = 2 ohms
I_T = 6 amperes   R3 = _____
R1 = 2 ohms   R4 = 2 ohms

6.

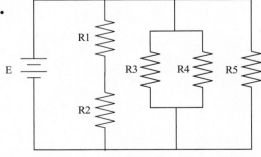

E = _____   R2 = 4 ohms   R5 = 4 ohms
I_T = 12 amperes   R3 = 16 ohms
R1 = 4 ohms   R4 = 16 ohms

67

Digital Multimeter Use for Electrical Problems

Meets NATEF Task: (A6-A-4) Demonstrate the proper use of a digital multimeter (DMM) during diagnosis of electrical circuit problems. (P-1)

Name _____ Date _____

Make/Model _____ Year _____ Instructor's OK [   ]

_____ **1.** Check service information on the correct procedure for checking charging system voltage.

_____

_____

       a. Which position on the digital multimeter should be selected to check charging system voltage.

          _____

          What is the specified voltage? _____

          What is the actual voltage? _____

       b. Which position should selected to check the voltage drop of the charging system? _____

          What is the specified voltage drop? _____

          What is the actual voltage drop? _____

_____ **2.** Check service information regarding the specified resistance for spark plug wires.

_____

       Which position on the DMM should be selected to measure spark plug wire resistance? _____

       What is the specified resistance? _____

       What is the actual (measured) resistance? _____

_____ **3.** Check service information regarding the specified battery drain test (parasitic draw) test procedures.

_____

       Which position on the DMM should be selected to measure battery electrical drain? _____

       What is the specified maximum battery electrical drain? _____

       What is the actual (measured) battery electrical drain? _____

68

Test Light Usage

Meets NATEF Task: (A6-A-6) Check electrical circuits with a test light; determine the necessary action. (P-2)

Name _____ Date _____

Make/Model _____ Year _____ Instructor's OK [____]

_____ 1. Check service information regarding which wire color(s) is the brake light and which is the tail light. Using a test light, check for voltage to the brake lights and tail lights at the rear of the vehicle.

_____

_____

    a. Brake light: _____ **OK** _____ **NOT OK** (describe fault) _____

_____

    b. Tail light: _____ **OK** _____ **NOT OK** (describe fault) _____

_____

_____ 2. Using a test light, check all of the fuses in the vehicle.

> ***NOTE:*** The ignition switch and/or lights need to be on to supply power to some fuses.

    List all good fuses: _____

_____

_____ 3. Based on the above activities, what is the necessary action? _____

_____

_____

_____

69

Circuit Testing Using a Fused Jumper Wire

Meets NATEF Task: (A6-A-7) Check electrical circuits using fused jumper wire; determine the necessary action. (P-2)

Name _____ Date _____

Make/Model _____ Year _____ Instructor's OK ☐

> *CAUTION:* A fused jumper wire should never be used to bypass an electrical load device.

_____ 1. Check service information for a diagnostic test procedure that includes the use of a fused jumper wire.

_____

_____

_____

_____ 2. A horn circuit is a commonly used circuit to show the use of a fused jumper wire.

a. Locate the horn (describe the location):

_____

b. Disconnect the wire from the horn.

c. Connect one end of the fused jumper wire to the terminal of the horn.

d. Touch the other end of the fused jumper wire to the positive (+) terminal of the battery.

e. The horn should work. **OK** _____ **NOT OK** _____

_____ 3. Based on the test results, what is the necessary action? _____

_____

70

Fusible Links, Circuit Breakers, and Fuses

Meets NATEF Task: (A6-A-9) Inspect and test fusible links, circuit breakers, and fuses; determine the necessary action. (P-1)

Name _____ Date _____

Make/Model _____ Year _____ Instructor's OK [　　]

_____ **1.** Check service information for the location procedures for all of the fusible links, circuit breakers, and fuses.

      A. Fusible links: Number _____   Location(s)_____

      B. Circuit breakers   Number _____   Location(s) _____

      C. Fuses   Number _____   Location(s)_____

_____ **2.** Describe the specified testing procedures.

      A. Fusible links _____

      B. Circuit breakers _____

      C. Fuses _____

NOTE: Many circuit breakers and fuses are not powered until the ignition switch is turned to the on (run) position or until the lights are turned on.

_____ **3.** Test the circuit protection devices.

      A. Fusible links   **OK** ____   **NOT OK** ____ (which ones?) _____

      B. Circuit breakers **OK** ____   **NOT OK** ____ (which ones?) _____

      C. Fuses   **OK** ____   **NOT OK** ____ (which ones?) _____

_____ **4.** Based on the tests, what is the necessary action?

      _____

      _____

      _____

71

Wire Repair

Meets NATEF Tasks: (A6-A-10 and A6-A-11) Remove and replace terminals, repair wiring harness, perform solder repair. (P-1s)

Name _____ Date _____

Make/Model _____ Year _____ Instructor's OK [   ]

_____ **1.** Check service information for the specified procedures to follow when performing a wire-related repair. List the specified procedures.

   _____

   _____

_____ **2.** Remove a terminal from a plastic connector. What tool was used to release the terminal from the connector?

   _____

_____ **3.** Perform a wire repair of a wiring harness. What method was used? Check all that apply.

   _____ Crimp and seal weather proof connectors

   _____ Solder and heat shrink tubing

   _____ Other (specify) _____

   Instructor OK _____

_____ **4.** Perform a solder repair of electrical wiring.

   Instructor OK _____

TOOL

AMP CONNECTOR

RAISING RETAINING FINGERS TO REMOVE CONTACTS

LOCKING WEDGE CONNECTOR

PLASTIC SPRING LATCHING TONGUE

PLASTIC SPRING LATCHING TONGUE

TANG CONNECTOR

SEAL

CRIMP CRIMP AND SOLDER

SEAL CORE CRIMP

72

Trace Electrical Circuits

Meets NATEF Task: (A6-A-3) Use wiring diagrams during diagnosis of electrical (electronic problems). (P-1)

Name _____ Date _____

Make/Model _____ Year _____ Instructor's OK ☐

_____ 1. Locate the wiring diagram (schematic) for the circuit being diagnosed. Describe the

circuit: _____

_____

_____ 2. Print out the wiring diagram and color all of the power side of the circuit red and the

ground side green.

_____ 3. The circuit is fed electrical power from what fusible link or mega fuse? _____

_____ 4. Check all that apply to the circuit below:

_____ Has a relay.

_____ The fuse feeds a single circuit.

_____ The fuse feeds more than one circuit.

_____ The ground is shared with another circuit.

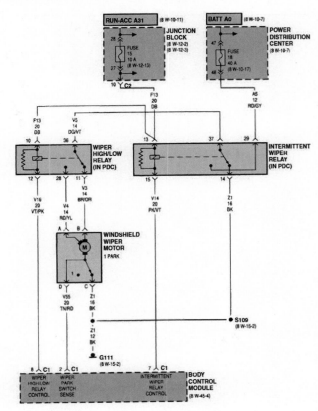

73

Key Off Battery Drain

Meets NATEF Task: (A6-A-8) Measure and diagnose the cause(s) of excessive key-off battery drain (parasitic draw); determine the necessary action. (P-1)

Name _____ Date _____

Make/Model _____ Year _____ Instructor's OK [   ]

A battery electrical drain test should be performed if a battery is dead (discharged) to determine if a battery electrical drain was the cause of the dead battery.

_____ 1. Perform a visual inspection and determine if any of the following circuits are on all the time.

        a. The glove box light (instrument panel compartment light)
        b. The interior light switch
        c. Vanity mirror(s) light(s)
        d. Underhood light
        e. Trunk light

_____ 2. Turn the ignition and all accessories off. Close all doors and the trunk. Disconnect the under-the-hood lamp if equipped.

_____ 3. Disconnect the negative (-) battery cable.

_____ 4. Select DC amperes on a digital multimeter.

_____ 5. Connect the black meter lead to the negative terminal of the battery.

_____ 6. Connect the red meter lead to the disconnected cable end and read the ammeter.

      _____ amps of battery electrical drain [should be less than 0.05A (50 mA)]

    OK _____   **NOT OK** _____

_____ 7. What is the necessary action? _____

_____

_____ 8. Reconnect the battery, reset the radio presets, and set the time on the vehicle clock.

> **HINT:** If possible, use a clip-on type digital multimeter or an amp probe to measure the battery drain. Using this equipment prevents the need to disconnect the battery cable and then have to reset the radio and the clock.

74

Battery Tests

Meets NATEF Task: (A6-B-1 and A6-B-2) Perform battery state-of-charge test; perform battery capacity test; determine necessary action. (P-1)

Name _____ Date _____

Make/Model _____ Year _____ Instructor's OK [   ]

_____ **1.** Check service information for the specified method for determining the state-of-charge and/or capacity test of the battery.

_____

_____

_____

_____ **2.** Determine the state-of-charge using a voltmeter.

12.6 volts or higher	= 100% charged
12.4 volts	= 75% charged
12.2 volts	= 50% charged
12.0 volts	= 25% charged
10.5 volts	= dead

_____ **3.** Determine the state-of-charge and capacity using a conductance tester.

_____

_____ **4.** Determine the capacity of the battery using a carbon pile tester.

_____

_____ **5.** What is the condition of the battery? _____

_____ **6.** What is the necessary action? _____

_____

75

Electronic Memory Saver Usage

Meets NATEF Task: (A6-B-3) Maintain or restore electronic memory functions. (P-1)

Name _____ Date _____

Make/Model _____ Year _____ Instructor's OK [　　]

_____ 1. Check service information for the specified method and tools or equipment needed to maintain or restore electronic memory function.

_____

_____

_____

_____ 2. Most domestic brand vehicles can use the cigarette (auxiliary outlet) to apply voltage when the battery of the vehicle is removed or disconnected during service. For this procedure to work, the lighter or auxiliary outlet must be powered with the ignition switch in the on position.

    a. Using a DMM set to read DC volts, check for battery voltage at the lighter socket with the ignition off. ____**OK** ____**NOT OK**

    b. Check for DC volts at the lighter socket with the ignition set to the on (run) position. ____ **OK** ____ **NOT OK**

_____ 3. If the vehicle is equipped with a top-post-type battery design, a jump box can be attached to the ends of the cables to keep the memory in the electronic components while the battery is removed. Is this a possible method?

    ____ Yes ____ No

_____ 4. Describe the method recommended to restore lost memory. _____

_____

_____

76

Inspect and Clean the Battery

Meets NATEF Task: (A6-B-4) Inspect, clean, fill, and replace the battery. (P-2)

Name _____ Date _____

Make/Model _____ Year _____ Instructor's OK [____]

_____ **1.** Check service information for the specified procedures to follow to inspect, clean, fill, and replace a battery.

_____

_____

_____ **2.** Check all that apply:

_____ Battery hold-down clamps/brackets are in place

_____ Filler cap(s) is removable

_____ Battery electrolyte cannot be checked

_____ Electrolyte level is low

_____ Corrosion was found on battery terminals/cable ends

_____ Other faults or conditions (describe)

_____

_____

_____ **3.** Clean the battery.

_____ **4.** Clean the battery cables and cable ends.

_____ **5.** Check the battery hold-downs.

77

Battery Charging

Meets NATEF Task: (A6-B-5) Perform slow/fast battery charge according to manufacturer's recommendations. (P-1)

Name _____ Date _____

Make/Model _____ Year _____ Instructor's OK [ ]

_____ **1.** Check service e information for the specified procedure to follow when changing a battery. Describe the specified procedure. _____
_____

_____ **2.** Percentage of charge = _____%.

        12.6 V or higher = 100% charged
        12.4 V   = 75% charged
        12.2 V   = 50% charged
        12.0 V   = 25% charged
        below 11.9 V   = discharged

_____ **3.** Determine the cold cranking amperes (CCA) of the battery = _____.

    (*The charge rate should be 1% of the CCA. For example, a battery with a 500 CCA rating should be charged at 5 ampere rate.*) Charge Rate = <u>CCA</u> 100

_____ **4.** Determine the reserve capacity in minutes = _____.

    (*The charge rate can be determined by dividing the reserve capacity of the battery in minutes by 30. For example, a 180-minute battery should be charged at 6 ampere rate: 180/30 = 6*).

$$\text{Charge Rate} = \frac{\text{Reserve Capacity}}{30}$$

_____ **5.** The battery should be charged at _____ amperes (CCA method) or at _____ amperes (reserve capacity method).

_____ **6.** Perform battery charge according to manufacturer's recommendation.

78

Jump Starting

Meets NATEF Task: (A6-B-6) Start a vehicle using jumper cables and a battery or auxiliary power supply. (P-1)

Name _____ Date _____

Make/Model _____ Year _____ Instructor's OK [   ]

_____ **1.** Move the good vehicle to within reach of the jumper cables of the disabled vehicle (or use a portable jumper box).

_____ **2.** Check that the ignition is in the "off" position on both vehicles.

_____ **3.** Connect the jumper cables in the following order:

      a. Red cable ends to the positive (+) terminals of both batteries
      b. One black cable end to the negative (-) terminal of the good vehicle
      c. The other black cable end to a good, unpainted engine ground at least one foot from the battery

_____ **4.** Start the good vehicle.

_____ **5.** Allow the good vehicle to run for several minutes to charge the battery of the disabled vehicle.

_____ **6.** Start the disabled vehicle.

_____ **7.** After the engine is running smoothly, disconnect the black cable from the engine ground of the disabled vehicle and then disconnect the negative terminal of the battery of the good vehicle.

_____ **8.** Disconnect the red battery cable ends from the positive terminals of the batteries.

79

Reinitialization

Meets NATEF Task: (A6-B-8) Identify electronic modules that require reinitialization or code entry following a battery disconnect. (P-2)

Name _____ **Date** _____

Make/Model _____ **Year** _____ **Instructor's OK** [ ]

_____ 1. Check service information for the electronic modules or components such as security radios that require reinitialization or code entry following a battery disconnect. Check all that apply.

      _____ Radio

      _____ Power windows

      _____ Power doors/taillights

      _____ Remote keyless entry

      _____ Security system

      _____ Other (specify) _____

_____ 2. What is the necessary action to reinitialize the electronic module?

Required procedure (in code entry)

Radio _____

Security system _____

Remote keyless entry _____

Power windows _____

Power doors/taillights _____

Security system _____

Other _____ _____

80

Hybrid Auxiliary Battery

Meets NATEF Task: (A6-B-9) Identify hybrid vehicle auxiliary (12V) battery service and test procedures. (P-3)

Name _____ **Date** _____

Make/Model _____ **Year** _____ **Instructor's OK** [ ]

_____ **1.** Check service information for the location of the hybrid vehicle auxiliary (12V)

battery _____

_____

_____ **2.** What are the battery specifications? CCA = _____ Size = _____

_____ **3.** Describe the service procedures: _____

_____

_____

_____ **4.** Based on the specified test results, what is the necessary action? _____

_____

_____

81

Inspect and Test Starter Switches and Connectors

Meets NATEF Task: (A6-C-5) Inspect and test switches, connectors, and wires of starter control circuit; determine necessary action. (P-2)

Name _____ Date _____

Make/Model _____ Year _____ Instructor's OK [ ]

_____ 1. Check service information for the specified procedure to follow when inspecting and testing starter control circuit switches, connectors, and wires. Describe the specified procedure _____

_____

_____

_____ 2. Check and test all connections that are used at the starter.

      _____ Positive battery cable

      _____ Fusible link

      _____ "S" terminal wire connection

      _____ Other (describe) _____

_____ 3. What is the condition of the starter control circuit wiring? Describe any faults:

_____

_____

_____ 4. If any faults are found, what is the necessary action: _____

_____

_____

82

Starter Relays and Solenoids

Meets NATEF Task: (A6-C-3 and A6-C-5) Inspect and test starter relays, solenoids, connections, and wires; determine necessary action. (P-2)

Name _____ Date _____

Make/Model _____ Year _____ Instructor's OK [ ]

_____ **1.** Clean and visually inspect the starter solenoid and/or relay for physical damage.

OK _____   NOT OK _____

_____ **2.** Set a digital multimeter (DMM) to read ohms (low scale) and check the hold-in coil and the pull-in coil.

Pull-in coil. Measure between terminals "S" and "M":
resistance = _____ (should be 0.2 to 0.4 ohm) **OK** _____ **NOT OK** _____

Hold-in coil. Measure between terminals "S" and the solenoid housing:
resistance = _____ (should be 0.4 to 0.6 ohm) **OK** _____ **NOT OK** _____

_____ **3.** Test the pull-in winding by applying 12 volts to terminal "S" and ground to terminal "M." Check that the plunger will be drawn into the solenoid.

OK _____   NOT OK _____

_____ **4.** Check the hold-in winding by connecting 12 volts to terminal "S" and the other wire to ground. The plunger should be drawn into the solenoid housing.

OK _____   NOT OK _____

_____ **5.** Measure coil resistance of the relay (terminals 86 and 85).

Resistance = _____ ohms
(should be 60 to 100 ohms)

OK _____   NOT OK _____

_____ **6.** What is the necessary action?

_____

_____

83

Starter Current Draw Test

Meets NATEF Task: (A6-C-1) Perform starter current draw tests; determine necessary action. Differentiate between electrical and engine mechanical problems. (P-1)

Name _____ Date _____

Make/Model _____ Year _____ Instructor's OK [   ]

_____ **1.** Check service information for the specified starter current draw test procedure and specifications and differentiate between electrical and engine mechanical problems.

_____

_____

NOTE: Few vehicle manufacturers give starter current draw specifications with the starter installed on the vehicle. Use the chart below as a guideline regarding the range of the maximum allowable starter draw.

4-cylinder engines = 150 to 185 amperes maximum
6-cylinder engines = 160 to 200 amperes maximum
8-cylinder engines = 185 to 250 amperes maximum

_____ **2.** Perform the starter current draw test following the manufacturer's instructions.

Results: _____ amperes

_____ **3.** Based on the specifications and the test results, what is the necessary action?

_____

_____

_____

_____

_____

84

Starter Circuit Voltage Drop

Meets NATEF Task: (A6-C-2) Perform starter circuit voltage drop tests; determine necessary action. (P-1)

Name _____ Date _____

Make/Model _____ Year _____ Instructor's OK [   ]

_____ **1.** Set the digital multimeter to DC volts.

> **HINT:** A voltmeter measures the difference in electrical pressure between the test leads. When the meter leads are connected to two locations and the engine is cranked, the meter will display the difference in voltage between the two points. This difference is called the voltage drop.

_____ **2.** Disable the ignition system or the fuel system to keep the engine from starting.

_____ **3.** Connect the voltmeter, as shown in the illustration, and crank the engine. Observe the voltmeter during each of the three tests.

_____ **4.** All test results should be less than 0.2 V (200 mV).

RESULTS:

_____ **ALL OK**
_____ **ALL NOT OK**

_____ **5.** Based on the results of the voltage drop tests, what is the necessary action?

_____

_____

85

Remove and Install the Starter

Meets NATEF Task: (A6-C-4) Remove and install starter in a vehicle. Inspect and test switches of the starter control circuit. (P-1)

Name _____ Date _____

Make/Model _____ Year _____ Instructor's OK [   ]

_____ **1.** Check service information for the specified procedures for the removal and installation of a starter in a vehicle.

_____

_____

_____

_____

_____ **2.** Does the service information require that the battery be disconnected? __ **Yes** __ **No**

_____ **3.** What are the torque specifications for the starter fasteners? _____

_____

_____ **4.** What is the condition of the connectors and wires of the starter control circuit? What is the necessary action? _____

_____

_____ **5.** Show the instructor the starter removed from the vehicle. **Instructor's OK** _____

_____ **6.** Show the instructor the starter installed in the vehicle. **Instructor's OK** _____

86

Alternator Drive Belt Inspection

Meets NATEF Task: (A6-D-3) Inspect alternator drive belt, pulley, and alignment. (P-1)

Name _____ **Date** _____

Make/Model _____ **Year** _____ **Instructor's OK** [ ]

_____ 1. Check service information for the specified procedure to follow when inspecting the alternator (generator) drive belt, pulley, and alignment. Describe the specified procedure. _____

_____

_____ 2. Describe the condition of the alternator drive belt and pulleys. _____

_____

_____ 3. Check alignment of the alternator drive belt. **OK** _____ **NOT OK** _____

_____ 4. Is the alternator equipped with an overrunning alternator pulley (OAP) or overrunning alternator dampener (OAD)? _____

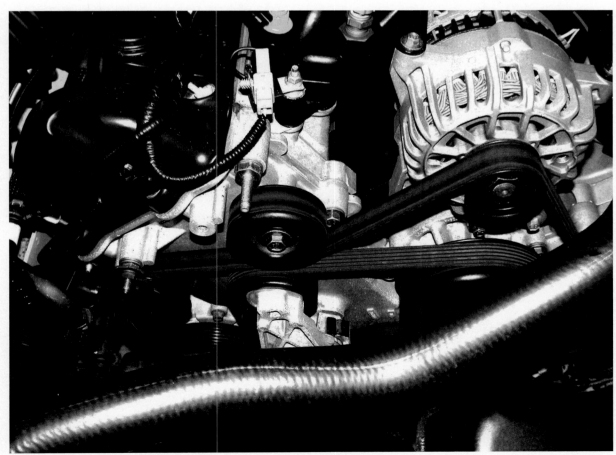

87

Charging System Output Test

Meets NATEF Task: (A6-D-1) Perform charging system output test; determine necessary action. (P-1)

Name _____ Date _____

Make/Model _____ Year _____ Instructor's OK [ ]

_____ **1.** Check service information for the specified charging system output test procedures and specifications.

_____

_____ **2.** Connect the starting and charging test unit (such as a Sun VAT-40) leads to the battery as per the manufacturer's instructions.

_____ **3.** Attach the amp probe around the alternator output wire.

_____ **4.** Start the engine and operate at 2,000 RPM (fast idle).

_____ **5.** Turn the "load increase" control slowly to obtain the highest reading on the ammeter scale. (Do not let the battery voltage drop to less than 12 volts.)
Tested amps = _____ amps.

_____ **6.** Specification (should be stamped on the alternator) or indicated by a colored tag on or near the output terminal) = _____ amps.

_____ **7.** Results should be within 10% of the specifications. If the alternator amperage output is low, first check the condition of the alternator drive belt. The alternator pulley should not be able to be rotated by hand with the engine "off."

         OK_____ NOT OK_____

_____ **8.** Based on the results of the charging system output test, what is the necessary action?

_____

_____

88

Charging Circuit Voltage Drop

Meets NATEF Task: (A6-D-4) Perform charging circuit voltage drop tests; determine necessary action (P-1)

Name _____ Date _____

Make/Model _____ Year _____ Instructor's OK [　　]

_____ **1.** Check service information for specified procedures and voltage drop specifications of the charging circuit.

_____ **2.** Connect one test lead of a digital multimeter set to read DC volts to the alternator output terminal and the positive (+) terminal of the battery.

_____ **3.** Start the engine and run to 2,000 RPM (fast idle).

_____ **4.** Turn on the headlights to force the alternator to charge the battery.

_____ **5.** The voltage drop reading should not exceed 0.40 volt.

    _____ = the voltage drop of the *insulated* (power side) of the charging circuit (between the output terminal of the alternator and the positive (+) terminal of the battery).

    OK_____ NOT OK_____

_____ **6.** To test if the alternator is properly grounded, continue operating the engine at a fast idle with the lights on, connect the meter leads to the case of the alternator and the negative (-) terminal of the battery. A reading of greater than 0.20 volt indicates a poor alternator ground.

    _____ = the voltage drop of the *ground side* of the alternator (between the rear housing of the alternator and the negative (-) terminal of the battery).

    OK_____ NOT OK_____

_____ **7.** Based on the test results, what is the necessary action? _____

_____

89

Remove and Install Generator (Alternator)

Meets NATEF Task: (A6-D-3) Remove, inspect, and install generator (alternator) and inspect drive belt. (P-1)

Name _____ Date _____

Make/Model _____ Year _____ Instructor's OK [ ]

_____ **1.** Check service information for the specified procedures for the removal and installation of a alternator in a vehicle.

_____

_____

_____

_____

_____

_____ **2.** Check condition of the drive belt and belt tension. __ **OK** __ **Not OK**

Describe faults: _____

_____ **3.** What are the torque specifications for the alternator fasteners? _____

_____

_____ **4.** What are the torque specifications for the wiring connectors? _____

_____

_____ **5.** Show the instructor the alternator removed from the vehicle. **Instructor's OK** _____

_____ **6.** Show the instructor the alternator installed in the vehicle. **Instructor's OK** _____

_____ **7.** Confirm proper alternator operation after installation.

90

Inspect Interior and Exterior Lamps

Meets NATEF Task: (A6-E-1) Inspect interior and exterior lamps and sockets; replace as needed. (P-1)

Name _____ **Date** _____

Make/Model _____ **Year** _____ **Instructor's OK** ☐

_____ 1. Check service information for the specified trade number of interior and exterior lamps. List the numbers for the following:

- Glove Box _____
- Courtesy lamp _____
- Brake lights _____
- Side marker lights _____
- Parking lights _____
- Trunk light _____
- License plate light _____

_____ 2. Check the operation of all interior and exterior lights. List those that need to be replaced. _____ _____ _____ _____

_____ 3. Does the socket require replacement in any of the lamps that did not work?

YES ---- NO ----

_____ 4. List all parts that were replaced. _____

_____

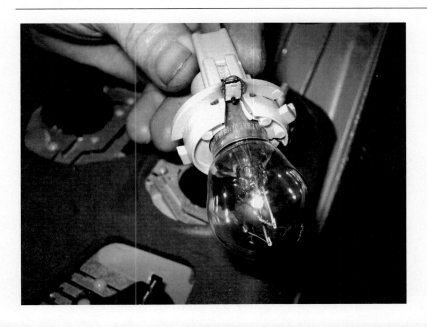

91

Headlight Replacement and Aiming

Meets NATEF Task: (A6-E-2) Inspect, replace, and aim headlights and bulbs.
(P-2)

Name _____ Date _____

Make/Model _____ Year _____ Instructor's OK [_____]

_____ 1. Check service information for the specified tools, equipment, and procedures to replace and aim headlights.

```
_____
_____
_____
_____
_____
_____
_____
_____
_____
_____
```

12 FEET (3.6 m) MINIMUM
DISTANCE BETWEEN HEADLAMPS
ADJUSTABLE VERTICAL TAPES
CENTER LINE OF SCREEN
HORIZONTAL CENTER LINE OF LAMPS
ADJUSTABLE HORIZONTAL TAPES
VEHICLE AXIS
25 FEET (7.6 m)
DIAGRAM OF LIGHT SCREEN
PAINTED REFERENCE LINE ON SHOP FLOOR

VERTICAL CENTERLINE AHEAD OF LEFT HEADLAMP | VEHICLE AXIS | VERTICAL CENTERLINE AHEAD OF RIGHT HEADLAMP | HEIGHT OF LAMP CENTERS | HIGH INTENSITY AREA | HIGH INTENSITY AREA
ADJUSTING PATTERN FOR LOW BEAM

VERTICAL CENTERLINE AHEAD OF LEFT HEADLAMP | VEHICLE AXIS | VERTICAL CENTERLINE AHEAD OF RIGHT HEADLAMP | HEIGHT OF LAMP CENTERS | HIGH INTENSITY AREA | HIGH INTENSITY AREA
ADJUSTING PATTERN FOR HIGH BEAM

_____ 2. What type of headlights are used on the vehicle?

_____ Sealed beam
_____ Halogen replacement bulbs
_____ High-intensity discharge (HID)
_____ Other (describe) _____

_____ 3. Is alignment equipment needed? ___ **Yes** ___ **No**

If yes, describe: _____

_____ 4. Is the headlight unit equipped with a bubble level? ___ **Yes** ___ **No**

92

High-Intensity Discharge Headlights

Meets NATEF Task: (A6-E-3) Identify system voltage and other precautions associated with HID headlights. (P-2)

Name _____ Date _____

Make/Model _____ Year _____ Instructor's OK ☐

_____ 1. Check service information for the specified precautions when working with high-intensity discharge (HID) lights. The safety precautions include:

      a. _____

      b. _____

      c. _____

_____ 2. What is the voltage output of the HID ballast assembly? _____

_____ 3. What is the specified testing procedure for diagnosing faults with high-intensity discharge lighting systems?

      Step 1: _____

      Step 2: _____

      Step 3: _____

      Step 4: _____

_____ 4. List the tools and test equipment needed to test high-intensity discharge headlight systems.

      a. _____

      b. _____

      c. _____

      d. _____

93

Brake Stop Light System

Meets NATEF Task: (A5-F-4) Check operation of the brake stop light system. (P-1)

Name _____ **Date** _____

Make/Model _____ **Year** _____ **Instructor's OK** [ ]

_____ **1.** Have an assistant depress the brake pedal and observe the brake lights for normal
operation.

     _____ **OK** (Functions correctly on both left and right sides.)

     _____ **NOT OK** (Brake lights do not work.)

     _____ **NOT OK** (describe the fault) _____

     _____

     _____

_____ **2.** Check service information and find the bulb trade number of the brake light bulbs.

     _____

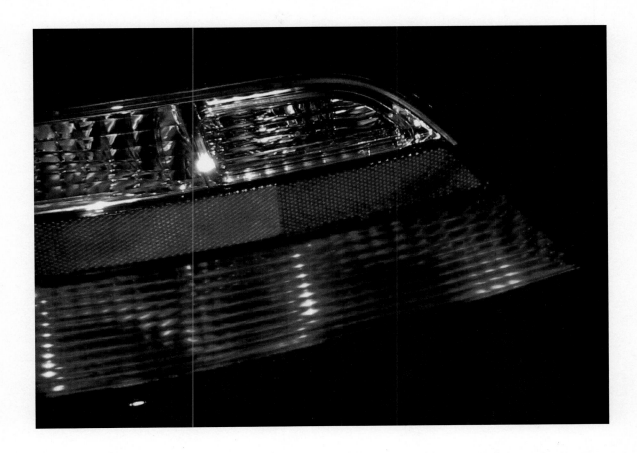

Brake Stop Light System

Worksheet 6A-10 (CBS 1-8) Check operation of the brake stop light system. (CBS...)

Name _____ Date _____

Make/Model _____ Year _____ Instructor's OK [ ]

1. Have an assistant depress the brake pedal and observe the brake lights for normal operation.

   OK (brakes operate correctly on both front and rear wheels)

   NOT OK (Brake lights do not work)

   NOT OK (describe the fault) _____

2. Check service information and find the bulb type number of the brake light bulb. _____

94

Reset Maintenance Indicators

Meets NATEF Task: (A1-A-2, A6-F-4) Verify operation of instrument panel gauges; reset maintenance indicator. (P-1)

Name _____ Date _____

Make/Model _____ Year _____ Instructor's OK [ ]

_____ 1. Check service information for the specified procedure to follow to reset maintenance indicators. Describe the specified procedure. _____

_____

_____

_____ 2. Verify the operation of all instrument panel gauges. Check all that apply:

       _____ Speedometer

       _____ Fuel gauge

       _____ Coolant temperature

       _____ Charging system

       _____ Brake warning light

       _____ Airbag light

       _____ Traction control

       _____ TPMS

       _____ Other (describe): _____

95

Wiper/Washer Operation/Wiper Blades

Meets NATEF Task: (A6-F-5) Verify windshield wipers/washers operation; replace wiper blades. (P-1)

Name _____ Date _____

Make/Model _____ Year _____ Instructor's OK ☐

_____ 1. Check service information for the specified procedure to follow when replacing windshield wiper blades. Describe the specified procedure: _____

_____

_____ 2. Check which procedure was specified:

      _____ Replace inserts

      _____ Replace wiper blades assembly

      _____ Other (describe) _____

           _____

_____ 3. Check operation of the windshield wipers and washers.

      _____ **OK** _____ **NOT OK** (describe fault) _____

_____ 4. Fill washer fluid with the specified fluid. Amount required = _____.

96

Door Panel

Meets NATEF Task: (A6-F-2) Remove and reinstall door panel. (P-1)

Name _____ **Date** _____

Make/Model _____ **Year** _____ **Instructor's OK** ☐

_____ **1.** Check service information for the specified procedures to follow to remove and

reinstall a door panel. _____

_____

_____ **2.** List the tools needed. _____

_____ **3.** Show the instructor the removed door panel. **Instructor's OK** _____

_____ **4.** How many clips and fasteners hold the door panel? _____

_____ **5.** Show the instructor the reinstalled door panel. **Instructor's OK** _____

97

Anti-Theft and Keyless Entry Systems

Meets NATEF Task: (A6-F-3) Diagnose problems with the anti-theft and keyless entry systems. (P-3)

Name _____ Date _____

Make/Model _____ Year _____ Instructor's OK [   ]

_____ **1.** Check service information for the specified testing procedures for the anti-theft

system. _____

_____

_____ **2.** List the tools and/or equipment needed or specified for the diagnosis of anti-theft

systems.

a. _____

b. _____

c. _____

d. _____

e. _____

f. _____

_____ **3.** Describe the operation of a keyless entry/remote start system.

_____

_____

_____

98

Airbag Disarming

Meets NATEF Task: (A4-A-2 and A6-F-1) Disarm and diagnose supplemental restraint systems; determine necessary action. (P-1s)

Name _____ Date _____

Make/Model _____ Year _____ Instructor's OK [   ]

_____ **1.** Check service information for specified disarming and enabling procedures. _____

_____

_____ **2.** Locate the airbag schematic and determine the following information.

    a. Describe the location of the airbag controller_____

    _____

    b. Describe the location of the arming sensor _____

    _____

    c. Describe the location of the discriminating sensors _____

    _____

_____ **3.** What fuse number (label) and amperage rating is used for the airbag?

    a. Fuse number (label) _____

    b. Fuse rating _____

_____ **4.** Describe the location of the ground(s) for the airbag. _____

    _____

_____ **5.** Based on the diagnostic tests, what is the necessary action? _____

_____

_____

99

Identify Air Conditioning Components

Meets NATEF Task: (A7-A-2) Identify air conditioning components. (P-1)

Name _____ Date _____

Make/Model _____ Year _____ Instructor's OK [ ]

_____ 1. Check service information for the names and location of the air conditioning components on the vehicle being inspected.

_____ 2. Describe the location of the following components:

- A/C compressor _____
- Evaporator _____
- Condenser _____
- Receiver/Drier/Accumulator _____
- High-side service fitting _____
- Low-side service fitting _____
- Expansion valve/Orifice tube _____

100

Inspect A/C Compressor Drive Belt

Meets NATEF Task: (A7-B-1) Inspect and replace A/C compressor drive belts, pulleys, and tensioner; determine necessary action. (P-1)

Name _____ Date _____

Make/Model _____ Year _____ Instructor's OK [   ]

_____ 1. Check service information for the specified procedure to follow to inspect and replace the A/C compressor drive belt, pulleys, and tensioners. Describe the specified procedures. _____

_____

_____

_____ 2. Describe the condition of the following items:

- A/C compressor drive belt _____
- A/C compressor drive belt pulleys _____
- A/C compressor drive belt tensioners _____

_____ 3. Based on the inspection, what is the necessary action? _____

_____

_____

101

Check A/C Condenser for Airflow Restriction

Meets NATEF Task: (A7-B-3) Inspect A/C condenser for airflow restrictions; perform necessary action. (P-1)

Name _____ **Date** _____

Make/Model _____ **Year** _____ **Instructor's OK** [ ]

_____ **1.** Check service information for the specified procedure to follow to get access to the condenser for inspection. Describe the procedure. _____

_____

_____ **2.** The specified procedure includes (check all that apply):

_____ Hoisting the vehicle

_____ Removing the grille

_____ Removing the air dam

_____ Other (specify) _____

_____ **3.** What is the specified method to use to clean the condenser? _____

_____

_____ **4.** Based on the inspection, what is the necessary action? _____

_____

_____

102

Cooling and Heater Hose Inspection

Meets NATEF Task: (A7-C-1) Inspect engine cooling and heater system hoses; perform necessary action. (P-1)

Name _____ Date _____

Make/Model _____ Year _____ Instructor's OK [　　]

_____ 1. Check service information for specified procedures to follow for inspecting engine cooling and heater system hoses. Describe specified procedure. _____

_____

_____

_____ 2. The specified inspection procedure includes the following (check all that apply).

_____ Visual inspection

_____ Pressure testing the cooling system

_____ Other (describe) _____

_____ 3. Based on the inspection, what is the necessary action? _____

_____

_____

103

Inspect Cabin Filter and A/C Ducts

Meets NATEF Task: (A7-D-1) Inspect A/C-heater ducts, doors, hoses, cabin filter, and outlets; perform necessary action. (P-1)

Name _____ Date _____

Make/Model _____ Year _____ Instructor's OK [ ]

_____ 1. Check service information for the specified procedure to follow to inspect the airflow ducts and cabin filter. Describe the specified procedure. _____

_____

_____ 2. Describe the location of the cabin filter: _____

_____

_____ 3. Check for proper airflow from the following vents (both left and right):

- Defroster **OK** ___ **NOT OK** ___

- Heater (floor vents) **OK** ___ **NOT OK** ___

- Dash vents **OK** ___ **NOT OK** ___

_____ 4. Based on the inspection, what is the necessary action? _____

_____

_____

104

Identify Source of A/C Odors

Meets NATEF Task: (A7-D-2) Identify source of A/C odors. (P-1)

___

Name _____ Date _____

Make/Model _____ Year _____ Instructor's OK [＿＿＿]

_____ 1. Check service information for the specified procedure to follow to determine and
correct A/C system odors. Describe the specified procedure. _____

_____

_____

_____ 2. Odors are usually caused by moisture and the growth of mold, mildew, fungi, bacteria,
as well as odors from food or smoking residue. The specified treatment includes
(check all that apply).

_____ Use of a deodorizer

_____ Installation of an "after blow" kit that keeps the blower motor operating for
several minutes after the engine has been stopped to dry out the
evaporator.

_____ Other (specify) _____

105

Hybrid Vehicle A/C System Precautions

Meets NATEF Task: (A7-B-1-2) Identify hybrid vehicle A/C system electrical circuits, service, and safety precautions. (P-3)

Name _____ Date _____

Make/Model _____ Year _____ Instructor's OK [ ]

_____ **1.** Check service information for the vehicle manufacturer's specified safety precautions regarding the A/C system electrical circuits, safety, and service.

    A. Electrical circuit precautions:

          _____

          _____

          _____

          _____

          _____

    B. Safety precautions: _____

          _____

          _____

    C. Service precautions: _____

          _____

          _____

          _____

          _____

106

Secondary Ignition Inspection and Testing

Meets NATEF Task: (A8-A-7) Inspect and test ignition primary and secondary circuit wiring and solid state components; test ignition coil(s); perform necessary action. (P-1)

Name _____ Date _____

Make/Model _____ Year _____ Instructor's OK [_____]

_____ 1. Check service information for the specifications and testing procedures for the secondary ignition wiring.

_____

_____ 2. Check coil output using a spark tester. **OK** _____ **NOT OK** _____

_____ 3. Carefully check the spark plug wire for damage or burned areas that could indicate a break in the insulation.

OK _____ **NOT OK** _____

_____ 4. Set the digital multimeter to read ohms (Ω).

_____ 5. List the length in feet and the resistance values in ohms for each spark plug wire according to the cylinder number:

	Length (feet)	Ohms
1.	_____	_____
2.	_____	_____
3.	_____	_____
4.	_____	_____
5.	_____	_____
6.	_____	_____
7.	_____	_____
8.	_____	_____

Coil wire: (if equipped)

_____ _____

_____ 6. Results - Original equipment radio suppression wires should test 10,000 ohms (10KΩ) or *less* per foot of length. **OK** _____ **NOT OK** _____

_____ 7. Based on the inspection and test(s), what is the necessary action? _____

_____

107

Spark Plugs Inspection

Meets NATEF Task: (A8-A-7) Inspect and test ignition primary and secondary circuit wiring and solid state components; test ignition coil(s); perform necessary action. (P-1)

Name _____ Date _____

Make/Model _____ Year _____ Instructor's OK [ ]

_____ 1. Check service information and determine the correct plug code and gap for your vehicle using a spark plug application guide.

Engine: # Cylinders_____ VIN# _____

Brand _____ Code # _____ Gap _____

_____ 2. Label and remove all the spark plug wires.

_____ 3. Determine the condition and gap of all spark plugs:

	Condition	Gap
1.	_____	_____
2.	_____	_____
3.	_____	_____
4.	_____	_____
5.	_____	_____
6.	_____	_____
7.	_____	_____
8.	_____	_____

_____ 4. Reinstall the spark plug (start by hand).

_____ 5. Use a torque wrench and torque the spark plugs to the proper torque.

Specified torque = _____

_____ 6. Start the engine. Check for possible rough running caused by crossed or loose spark plug wires.

OK _____ **NOT OK** _____

_____ 7. Based on the inspection of the spark plugs, what is the necessary action? _____

_____

108

Replace Fuel Filter

Meets NATEF Task: (A8-C-1) Replace the fuel filter. (P-1)

Name _____ Date _____

Make/Model _____ Year _____ Instructor's OK ☐

_____ 1. Check service information for the specified procedure to follow when replacing the fuel filter. Describe the specified procedure. _____

_____

_____

_____ 2. Where is the fuel filter located?

_____ Inside the fuel tank (usually not a replaceable type filter)

_____ Under the vehicle in the fuel line

_____ Other (describe) _____

_____ 3. What is the specified fuel filter replacement interval? _____

_____

109

We Support
NATEF
ASE CERTIFIED

Air Intake Inspection

Meets NATEF Task: (A8-C-2) Inspect, service, or replace air filters, filter housings, and intake duct work. (P-1)

Name _____ **Date** _____

Make/Model _____ **Year** _____ **Instructor's OK** [ ]

_____ **1.** Check service information for the specified procedure to follow when inspecting the air filter housing and intake duct work. Describe specified procedure. _____

_____

_____

_____ **2.** Is the vehicle equipped with an airflow meter that turns red when the filter is restricted?

　　　　　_____ **Yes** (describe condition) _____

　　　　　_____ **No**

_____ **3.** Inspect the area where the air enters the intake duct for restrictions. Describe the results. _____

_____

_____

110

PCV System Inspection

Meets NATEF Task: (A8-D-1) Inspect, test, and service positive crankcase ventilation (PCV) filter/breather cap, valve, tubes, orifices and hoses; perform necessary action. (P-2)

Name _____   Date _____

Make/Model _____   Year _____   Instructor's OK [   ]

_____ **1.** Check service information for the recommended steps to follow when testing or servicing the positive crankcase ventilation (PCV) system.

_____

_____

_____ **2.** Check service information and describe the location of the following:

PCV valve _____

Crankcase vent filter _____

Fixed orifice (if equipped) _____

Tubes _____

Other (describe) _____

_____ **3.** What is specified replacement interval for the PCV valve?

_____

_____ **4.** Remove and clear the PCV valve (if equipped) and note the condition.

_____ Like new   _____ Very dirty

_____ Slightly dirty   _____ Valve clogged or stuck

_____ Other (describe) _____

_____ **5.** Based on the test and inspection and on the recommendation of the vehicle manufacturer, what is the necessary action?

_____

111

Hybrid Vehicle 12-Volt Auxiliary Battery Service

Meets NATEF Task: (A6-B-9) Identify hybrid 12-volt auxiliary battery service, repair, and test procedures. (P-3)

Name _____ Date _____

Make/Model _____ Year _____ Instructor's OK [ ]

_____ 1. Check service information for the specified testing and service procedures to follow when working with a 12-volt auxiliary battery on a hybrid electric vehicle. Describe the specified procedures. _____

_____

_____

_____ 2. Locate the 12-volt auxiliary battery. Check the following that best describes its Location.

        _____ Under the hood

        _____ Behind the rear seat

        _____ In the trunk

        _____ Other (describe) _____

_____ 3. What is the type of this 12-volt battery?

        _____ Flooded type

        _____ Absorbed glass mat (AGM)

112

Regenerative Braking System

Meets NATEF Task: (A5-G-2) Describe the operation of a regenerative braking system. (P-3)

Name _____ **Date** _____

Make/Model _____ **Year** _____ **Instructor's OK** [ ]

_____ 1. Search service information for a hybrid electric or electric vehicle that uses regenerative brakes to determine how they operate. Describe how they operate.

_____

_____

_____

_____

_____ 2. Check service information for the precautions needed when servicing the brakes on a vehicle equipped with a regenerative braking system. List the precautions.

    A. _____

    B. _____

    C. _____

Regenerative Braking System

Meets NATEF Task: (A6-D-7) Describe the operation of a regenerative braking system. (P-3)

Name _____ Date _____

Make/Model _____ Year _____ Instructor's OK ☐

1. Supply service information (URL) here or electronic data _____ to generally brakes to determine how they operate. Describe how they operate.

2. Check service information for the precautions needed when servicing the brakes and vehicles equipped with a regenerative braking system. List the precautions.

113

OBD II Monitors

Meets NATEF Task: (A8-B-2) Describe the importance of the OBD II monitors for repair verification. (P-1)

Name _____ **Date** _____

Make/Model _____ **Year** _____ **Instructor's OK** [ ]

_____ 1. Connect a scan tool to the data link connector (DLC) and determine which monitors are active on the vehicle being tested. Check all that are ready or complete.

____ Catalytic converter	____ A/C refrigerant
____ EVAP	____ Comprehensive component
____ Oxygen sensor	____ Fuel system
____ HO2S heater	____ Misfire
____ EGR	____ Secondary air injection (AIR)
____ Heated catalyst	

_____ 2. Check service information to determine what the criteria is (tests needed to pass) for the monitor to run and pass? Describe the requirements. _____

_____

_____

_____ 3. Explain why having the monitors run and pass verifies that a repair performed was successful. _____

_____

_____

```
     TEST RESULTS
  ==========================
 eadiness Test (Mode 1):
 /C Sys Refrigerant:      Not Available
 atalyst:                 Ready
 Comprehensive Comp:      Ready
 EGR System:              Not Available
 Evaporative System:      Ready
 Fuel System:             Ready
 Heated Catalyst:         Not Available
 Misfire Monitor:         Ready
```

114

Scan Tool Diagnosis

Meets NATEF Task: (A8-B-1) Retrieve and record stored OBD II diagnostic trouble codes; clear codes. (P-1)

Name _____ Date _____

Make/Model _____ Year _____ Instructor's OK [＿＿]

_____ **1.** Check service information for the specified method for retrieving diagnostic trouble codes on the OBD II vehicle being serviced.

　　　　_____

　　　　_____

_____ **2.** Set a diagnostic trouble code by unplugging a component that is checked by the comprehensive component monitor (CCM), such as the throttle position sensor.

EXAMPLE: P0302 = CYLINDER #2 MISFIRE DETECTED

P 0 3 0 2

B - BODY
C - CHASSIS
P - POWER TRAIN
U - NETWORK

0 - GENERIC (SAE)
1 - MANUFACTURER SPECIFIC

SPECIFIC FAULT DESIGNATION

SPECIFIC VEHICLE SYSTEM

_____ **3.** Retrieve and record the stored diagnostic trouble code (DTC).

　　　　Which code(s) was set? _____

_____ **4.** Using specified testing procedures, what system is at fault? _____

　　　　_____

_____ **5.** Clear the codes. Describe the procedure used. _____

　　　　_____

　　　　_____

Tire Information

Meets NATEF Task: (Task Not Specified by NATEF for MLR)

Name _____ Date _____

Make/Model _____ Year _____ Instructor's OK ☐

_____ **1.** Check service information and determine the following tire-related information.

    A. Tire size _____

    B. Spare tire size _____

    C. Specified inflation pressure _____

    D. Spare tire inflation pressure _____

    E. Optional tire size (if any) _____

_____ **2.** Check service information and determine the following tire service-related information.

    A. Recommended tire rotation method: _____

    _____

    _____

    B. Recommended tire rotation mileage: _____

    _____

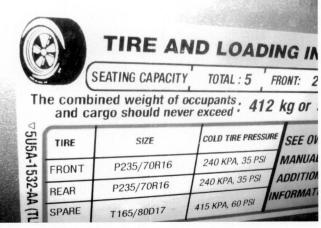

TIRE AND LOADING IN

SEATING CAPACITY   TOTAL : 5   FRONT: 2

The combined weight of occupants and cargo should never exceed : **412 kg or**

TIRE	SIZE	COLD TIRE PRESSURE	SEE OV
FRONT	P235/70R16	240 KPA, 35 PSI	MANUAL
REAR	P235/70R16	240 KPA, 35 PSI	ADDITION
SPARE	T165/80D17	415 KPA, 60 PSI	INFORMAT

5U5A-1532-AA (TL

116

Tire Pressure Monitoring System

Meets NATEF Task: (A4-D-7) Inspect, diagnose and calibrate tire pressure monitoring system. (P-2)

Name _____ **Date** _____

Make/Model _____ **Year** _____ **Instructor's OK** [_____]

_____ **1.** Check service information to determine the specified procedure to follow when inspecting, diagnosing, or calibrating the tire pressure monitoring system. Describe the specified procedures.

_____

_____

_____

_____ **2.** With what type of TPMS is the vehicle equipped?

    _____ Indirect

    _____ Direct

    If direct-type system, what type of sensor is used?

        _____ Stem-mounted

        _____ Banded

        _____ Unknown

_____ **3.** Is recalibrating the sensors needed if the tires are rotated?

    _____ Yes (If yes, what is the procedure?) _____

_____

    _____ No

117

Tire Inspection and Air Loss

Meets NATEF Task: (A4-D-1 and A4-D-5) Inspect tire condition and check for loss of air pressure. (P-1)

Name _____ Date _____

Make/Model _____ Year _____ Instructor's OK [ ]

_____ **1.** Inspect tire condition and inflation pressure. Record the results:

	Condition	Tread Depth	Inflation Pressure
Left front	_____	_____	_____
Right front	_____	_____	_____
Right rear	_____	_____	_____
Left rear	_____	_____	_____
Spare	_____	_____	_____

_____ **2.** Check tires for air loss. Describe the procedure used. _____

_____

_____ **3.** Based on the inspection results, what is the necessary action? _____

_____

_____

TIRE TREAD

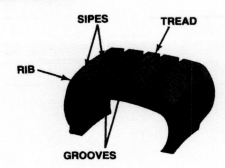

SIPES   TREAD

RIB

GROOVES

118

Tire Rotation

Meets NATEF Tasks: (A4-D-2) Rotate tires according to manufacturer's recommendations. (P-1)

Name _____ Date _____

Make/Model _____ Year _____ Instructor's OK [   ]

_____ 1. Check the service information for the recommended tire rotation method.

_____ Cannot rotate tires on this vehicle
_____ Modified X method
_____ X method
_____ Front to rear and rear to front

FRONT-WHEEL DRIVE   REAR-WHEEL DRIVE

FRONT   FRONT

MODIFIED "X"
(PREFERRED METHOD)

_____ 2. Hoist the vehicle safely to a good working position (chest level).

_____ 3. Remove the wheels and rotate them (if possible) according to the vehicle manufacturer's recommendation.

FRONT-OR
REAR-WHEEL DRIVE   FRONT-OR
REAR-WHEEL DRIVE

FRONT   FRONT

_____ 4. Check and correct the tire air pressures according to the service information on the placard on the driver's door.

Specified front tire air pressure = _____

Specified rear tire air pressure = _____

FULL "X"
(ACCEPTABLE)   FRONT/REAR
(ACCEPTABLE)

_____ 5. Torque lug nut to factory specification (specify)

_____

_____ 6. Lower the vehicle and move the hoist pads before driving the vehicle out of the service stall.

119

Install Wheel on Vehicle

Meets NATEF Task: (A5-C-6) Reinstall wheel; torque lug nuts.
(P-1)

Name _____ Date _____

Make/Model _____ Year _____ Instructor's OK [ ]

_____ **1.** Determine the vehicle manufacturer's specified lug nut torque specification.

_____ (usually between 80 and 100 lb-ft)

_____ **2.** Use a hand-operated wire brush on the wheel studs to ensure clean and dry threads and check for damage.

OK _____ **NOT OK** _____ Describe fault: _____

_____ **3.** Verify that the lug nuts are OK and free of defects.

> *CAUTION:* Some vehicle manufacturers warn to not lubricate the wheel studs because this can cause the lug nuts to loosen while the vehicle is being driven, resulting in personal injury.

_____ **4.** Install the wheel over the studs and start all lug nuts (or bolts) by hand.

_____ **5.** Tighten the lug nuts a little at a time in a star pattern using an air impact wrench equipped with the proper torque limiting adapter or a torque wrench.

_____ Used a torque wrench

_____ Used an air impact with a torque limiting adapter

_____ **6.** Tighten the lug nuts to final torque in a star pattern.

> *NOTE:* "Tighten one, skip one, tighten one" is the usual method if four or five lug nuts are used.

120

Tire Replacement

Meets NATEF Task: (A4-D-3, A4-D-4, A4-D-8) Dismount and remount tire on wheel; balance wheel tire and assembly. (P-1, P-2, P-2)

Name _____ Date _____

Make/Model _____ Year _____ Instructor's OK [   ]

_____ **1.** Check the instructions for the proper use of the tire changer. Describe the recommended procedure.

_____

_____

_____ **2.** Check all steps that were performed.

       _____ Removed the valve core (TPMS equipped tire/wheel assembly; check service information for the exact procedure to follow.)

INSTALL TPMS SENSOR
FLAT SIDE DOWN

       _____ Demount the tire from the wheel. **Instructor OK** _____

       _____ Clean bead seat.

       _____ Lubricate the tire bead.

       _____ Mount the tire and inflate to specified inflation pressure.

_____ **3.** Balance tire/wheel assembly.

       Instructor OK _____

121

Tire Repair

Meets NATEF Task: (A4-D-6) Repair tire using internal patch. (P-1)

Name _____ Date _____

Make/Model _____ Year _____ Instructor's OK [   ]

_____ 1. Locate the source of the leak by submerging the tire under water or by spraying the
tire with soapy water. Describe the location of the leak.

> **NOTE:** Sidewall punctures are not repairable. Repair a tire only if the leak is
> located in the tread area.

_____

_____ 2. Remove the foreign object and use a reamer to clean
the hole in the tire.

_____ 3. Dismount the tire and buff the inside of the tire
around the hole.

_____ 4. Apply rubber cement to the buffed area as per
the instructions.

_____ 5. Insert the repair plug from the inside of the tire.

_____ 6. Pull the plug through the puncture from the outside of the tire.

_____ 7. Use a stitching tool to make sure the inside of the patch is well adhered to the inside of
the tire.

_____ 8. Remount the tire and inflate to the air pressure specified by the vehicle manufacturer.

_____ 9. Check the repair for air leaks using soapy water.

       OK _____ **NOT OK** _____

122

Inspect Control Arms and Jounce Bumpers

Meets NATEF Task: (A4-B-10, A4-B-11, and A4-B-12) Inspect control arms/bushings and jounce bumpers. (P-1)

Name _____ Date _____

Make/Model _____ Year _____ Instructor's OK [ ]

_____ 1. Check service information for the specified procedure to follow when inspecting control arms and control arm bushings. Describe specified procedure. _____

_____

_____

_____ 2. Describe specified procedure to follow when inspecting jounce (rebound) bumpers.

_____

_____

_____ 3. Inspect track rod and radius rods and bushings. **OK ___ NOT OK ___**

123

Ball Joint Inspection

Meets NATEF Task: (A4-B-13) Inspect upper and lower ball joints (with and without wear indicator. (P-1)

Name _____ **Date** _____

Make/Model _____ **Year** _____ **Instructor's OK** ☐

_____ **1.** Check service information for the specified method and procedure to use to check upper and lower ball joints. Describe specified procedures. _____

_____

_____

_____

_____ **2.** What type of ball joint is being tested?

       Upper   _____ indicator   _____ non-indicator

       Lower   _____ indicator   _____ non-indicator

_____ **3.** What was the result of the inspection? _____

_____

_____

_____

124

Inspect Coil Springs and Torsion Bars

Meets NATEF Task: (A4-B-14 and A4-B-15) Inspect suspension coil springs and torsion bars.
(P-1)

Name _____ **Date** _____

Make/Model _____ **Year** _____ **Instructor's OK** ☐

_____ **1.** Check service information for the specified procedure to follow when inspecting coil
springs and spring insulators (silencers). Describe the specified procedures.

_____

_____

_____

_____

_____

_____

_____

_____ **2.** Check service information for the specified procedures to follow when inspecting
torsion bars and mounts. Describe specified procedures. _____

_____

_____

_____

125

Front Stabilizer Bar Bushings/Links

Meets NATEF Task: (A4-B-16) Inspect and replace front stabilizer bar (sway bar) bushings, brackets, and links. (P-1)

Name _____ Date _____

Make/Model _____ Year _____ Instructor's OK [ ]

_____ 1. Check service information for the specified procedures to follow when inspecting and replacing stabilizer bar bushings and links. Describe specified procedures.

_____

_____

_____ 2. Based on the inspection, what parts need to be replaced? Check all that apply.

_____ Stabilizer bar

_____ Stabilizer bar mounting bushings

_____ Stabilizer bar brackets

_____ Stabilizer bar links

_____ 3. What is the specified procedure to follow when replacing the part? Describe. _____

_____

_____

_____

126

Inspect Strut and Bearing

Meets NATEF Task: (A4-B-17 and A4-B-18) Inspect strut cartridge/assembly and strut bearing/mount). (P-1)

Name _____ Date _____

Make/Model _____ Year _____ Instructor's OK [____]

_____ **1.** Check service information for the specified procedure to follow when inspecting a strut assembly. Describe specific procedure. _____

_____

_____

_____ **2.** Check fault found:

    _____ OK – no faults found

    _____ Leaking strut

    _____ Worn/noisy upper mount

    _____ Worn lower mount

    _____ Other (describe) _____

127

Inspect and Replace Shock Absorbers

Meets NATEF Task: (A4-B-21) Inspect and replace shock absorbers; inspect mounts and bushings. (P-1)

Name _____ **Date** _____

Make/Model _____ **Year** _____ **Instructor's OK** [＿＿＿]

_____ 1. Check service information for the specified procedure to follow when inspecting and
replacing shock absorbers. Describe the specified procedure. _____

_____

_____

_____ 2. Describe the results of the inspection of the shock mounts and bushings. Check all
that apply.

Front shocks: Left _____ OK _____ NOT OK

Right _____ OK _____ NOT OK

Rear shocks: Left _____ OK _____ NOT OK

Right _____ OK _____ NOT OK

_____ 3. What shocks were replaced?

_____ Both front shocks

_____ Both rear shocks

128

We Support NATEF

Inspect Rear Suspension Leaf Springs and Arms

Meets NATEF Task: (A4-B-19 and A4-B-20) Inspect rear suspension links/arms and leaf springs. (P-1)

Name _____ **Date** _____

Make/Model _____ **Year** _____ **Instructor's OK** ☐

_____ 1. Check service information for the specified procedures to follow when inspecting rear suspension links/arms. Describe specified procedures. _____

_____

_____

_____ 2. Check service information for the specified procedure to follow when inspecting rear leaf springs, spring insulators (silencers), shackles, brackets, bushings, center pin/bolts and mounts. Describe specified procedure. _____

_____

_____

_____ 3. What was the result of the inspection? Describe the condition of the rear suspension links/arms and leaf springs. _____

_____

_____

129

Inspect Steering Linkage Components

Meets NATEF Task: (A4-B-1, A4-B-8, A4-B-9) Inspect pitman arm, relay rod, idler arm, and tie rod ends. (P-1)

Name _____ Date _____

Make/Model _____ Year _____ Instructor's OK [＿＿＿]

_____ 1. Check service information for the specified procedure to follow when inspecting steering linkage components. Describe specified procedure. _____

_____

_____

_____ 2. What type of steering system is being checked?

_____ Parallelogram

_____ Cross-steer

_____ Holtenberger

_____ Rack and pinion

_____ 3. Describe the condition of the inspected steering components. _____

_____

_____

130

Power Steering System Service

Meets NATEF Task: (A4-B-2 through A4-B-7 and A4-B-24) Inspect power steering system including power steering fluid replacement, bleeding, filter, and drive belt. (P-1)

Name _____ Date _____

Make/Model _____ Year _____ Instructor's OK [＿＿]

_____ 1. Check service information for the specified fluid and service procedures to follow when servicing a power steering system. List the specified items.

- Type of fluid _____

_____

- Specified procedure for hose replacement _____

_____

- Procedure for bleeding _____

_____

- Location of power steering filter (if equipped) _____

_____

- Procedure for leak checking _____

_____

_____ 2. Check the condition of the power steering pump drive belt. Describe the condition.

_____

_____

131

Electric Power Steering Service

Meets NATEF Task: (A4-B-22 and A4-B-23) Inspect electric power steering system and identify electrical circuit and safety precautions. (P-2)

Name _____ **Date** _____

Make/Model _____ **Year** _____ **Instructor's OK** ☐

_____ 1. Check service information regarding the parts and operation of the electric power steering system and identify the location of the following components. Check type.

　　　_____ Column mounted _____

　　　_____ Pinion mounted _____

　　　_____ Rack mounted _____

_____ 2. Describe the location of the following components.

　　　Power steering control module _____

　　　Power steering motor assembly _____

　　　Steering wheel position sensor _____

_____ 3. Check service information and determine the electric power steering system electrical circuits and safety precautions on a hybrid and non-hybrid electric vehicle. _____

_____

_____

132

Pre-Alignment Inspection

Meets NATEF Task: (A4-C-1) Perform prealignment inspection and measure vehicle ride height; perform necessary action. (P-1)

Name _____ Date _____

Make/Model _____ Year _____ Instructor's OK [ ]

_____ 1. Check service information for the specified tests and procedures to follow when performing a pre-alignment inspection. Describe the specified procedures.

_____

_____

_____ 2. Check tires. Both front tires and both rear tires should be checked for the following:

    A. Correct tire pressure

    B. Same size and brand

    C. Same tread depth

    OK _____   **NOT OK** _____

_____ 3. Perform a dry-park test to check for any looseness in the steering and suspension components such as:

    A. Tie rods

    B. Idler arms

    C. Ball-joints

    D. Control arm bushings

    E. Loose or defective wheel bearings

    OK _____   **NOT OK** _____

_____ 4. Check for proper ride height.

    A. Front and rear

    B. Left and right

    OK _____   **NOT OK** _____

133

Brake System Operation Road Test

Meets NATEF Task: (A5-A-2) Describe procedure for performing a road test to check brake system operation. (P-1)

Name _____ Date _____

Make/Model _____ Year _____ Instructor's OK [   ]

_____ 1. Check service information for the specified procedure to follow when performing a road test to check for proper brake system operation. Describe the specified procedure. _____

_____

CAUTION: Do not perform a road test if the red brake warning lamp is on.

_____ 2. What was discovered during the test drive? Check all that apply.

_____ Normal operation

_____ Noise during braking

_____ Pulls to one side during braking _____ Left _____ Right

_____ Low brake pedal

_____ Warning lamp comes on during braking

_____ Other (describe) _____

134

Traction Control/Stability Control Components

Meets NATEF Task: (A5-G-1) Identify traction control/vehicle stability control system components. (P-3)

Name _____ Date _____

Make/Model _____ Year _____ **Instructor's OK** ☐

_____ 1. Check service information and reference materials and describe the components used as part of the traction control/vehicle stability control system. Describe the components involved. _____

_____

_____

_____ 2. Check all that are used for traction control/vehicle stability control.

_____ Traction control/vehicle stability warning light

_____ ABS wheel speed sensors

_____ Steering wheel (handwheel) position sensor

_____ Yaw sensor

_____ Electrohydraulic control unit

_____ Electronic brake controller (computer)

_____ Other (describe) _____

_____

135

Brake Pedal Height

Meet NATEF Task: (A5-B-1) Measure brake pedal height; determine necessary action. (P-1)

Name _____ Date _____

Make/Model _____ Year _____ Instructor's OK [　　]

_____ 1. State the vehicle manufacturer's specified brake height testing procedure:

_____

_____

_____

_____ 2. Measure the brake pedal height from the bottom
of the steering wheel or floor to the brake pedal.

_____ = inch (cm)

_____ 3. Depress the brake pedal until the brakes are
applied and measure the brake pedal height.

_____ = inch (cm)

_____ 4. Subtract the second reading from the first
reading. This is the brake pedal travel.

_____ = brake pedal travel (should be a maximum of 2.0 to 2.5 in.)

_____ 5. List three items that could cause a greater than normal brake pedal travel.

A. _____

B. _____

C. _____

_____ 6. Based on the test results, what is the necessary action: _____

_____

136

Master Cylinder

Meet NATEF Task: (A5-B-2) Check master cylinder for external and internal leaks and proper operation. (P-1)

Name _____ Date _____

Make/Model _____ Year _____ Instructor's OK [　　]

_____ **1.** Check visually for signs of external brake fluid leaks.

      _____ **OK** _____ **NOT OK**

      Describe location _____

_____ **2.** Check for internal leakage by observing the level of brake fluid in the front compared to the rear.

      A. Is the level higher in the front than the rear? _____ **Yes** _____ **No**

      B. Is the brake pedal lower than normal? _____ **Yes** _____ **No**

      If yes to both A and B above, then the master cylinder is leaking internally and must be replaced.

_____ **3.** Press on the brake pedal with the engine running in Park. Does the pedal slowly drop down? If so, and there are no signs of external leaks, the master cylinder is leaking internally and needs service.

_____ **4.** Have an assistant depress the brake pedal while watching the brake fluid in the master cylinder reservoir. The brake fluid should be seen to move as the brake pedal is being depressed if the sealing caps are OK and positioned correctly.

      Movement observed? _____ **Yes** _____ **No**

      If brake fluid does not move and there is a breaking system problem, the master cylinder or linkage adjustment is faulty.

_____ **5.** Based on the test results, what is the necessary action? _____

_____

137

Brake Warning Light System

Meets NATEF Task: (A5-B-5) Identify components of the brake warning light system. (P-3)

Name _____ **Date** _____

Make/Model _____ **Year** _____ **Instructor's OK** ☐

_____ **1.** Check service information for the exact components involved in the brake warning
light system on the vehicle being checked. Check all that apply.

     _____ Brake fluid level sensor

     _____ Differential pressure switch

     _____ Parking brake switch

_____ **2.** Is the brake warning light system working as designed?

     _____ Yes   _____ No

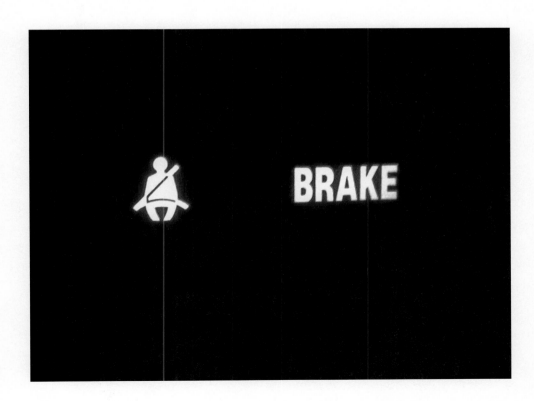

138

Brake Hose and Line Inspection

Meet NATEF Task: (A5-B-3) Inspect brake lines and flexible hose for faults and determine necessary action. (P-1)

Name _____ Date _____

Make/Model _____ Year _____ Instructor's OK [   ]

_____ **1.** Hoist the vehicle safely.

_____ **2.** Remove all four wheels.

_____ **3.** Carefully inspect the flexible brake hoses on the
left front, right front, and rear (one or two
flexible hoses) for the following:

　　　　_____ Leaks **OK** ___ **NOT OK** ___ Which hose(s)? _____

　　　　_____ Kinks **OK** ___ **NOT OK** ___ Which hose(s)? _____

　　　　_____ Cracks **OK** ___ **NOT OK** ___ Which hose(s)? _____

　　　　_____ Bulges or wear **OK** ___ **NOT OK** ___ Which hose(s)? _____

_____ **4.** Carefully inspect the steel brake lines from the master cylinder to the junction with the
flexible brake lines and check for the following:

　　　　_____ Leaks **OK** ___ **NOT OK** ___ Fault location? _____

　　　　_____ Dents **OK** ___ **NOT OK** ___ Fault location? _____

　　　　_____ Loose fittings or supports **OK** ___ **NOT OK** ___

　　　　Fault location? _____

_____ **5.** Based on the inspection, what is the necessary action? _____

　　　　_____

　　　　_____

139

Brake Fluid

Meet NATEF Task: (A5-B-4) Select, handle, store, and fill brake fluids to proper level. (P-1)

Name _____ Date _____

Make/Model _____ Year _____ Instructor's OK [   ]

_____ 1. Consult the vehicle manufacturer's service information and determine the specified type of brake fluid.

       ____ DOT 3   ____ DOT 4   ____ Other (specify) _____

_____ 2. All brake fluid should be stored in a sealed container. Specify what type and size container of container is being used.

       _____ Metal (preferred because air containing moisture cannot penetrate metal)

       _____ Plastic (makes shelf life shorter because air containing moisture can penetrate most plastic)

       _____ Size (number of ounces or ml) _____

_____ 3. Brake fluid can remove paint so protective covers should be used whenever handling brake fluid. Check all that should be done when handling brake fluid.

       _____ Use fender covers

       _____ Wear protective gloves

_____ 4. Fill brake fluid to the "MAX" line on the master cylinder reservoir.

> *CAUTION:* If the brake fluid level is too high, the brakes may self-apply when the normal operation of the wheel brakes warms the brake fluid, which expands in volume. If the brake fluid is unable to expand in the master cylinder reservoir, the pressure increases and the brakes can be applied even though the driver did not depress the brake pedal.

140

Brake Fluid Contamination Test

Meets NATEF Task: (A5-B-7) Test brake fluid for contamination. (P-1)

Name _____ Date _____

Make/Model _____ Year _____ Instructor's OK [   ]

_____ **1.** Check service information for the procedure to follow when checking brake fluid for contamination. Describe specified instructions:

_____

_____

_____ **2.** What method was used to test brake fluid for contamination? (check all that apply)

_____ Test strips

_____ Electronic boiling point tester

_____ Placed brake fluid in a Styrofoam cup and checked for a ring indicating mineral oil was in the brake fluid

_____ Allowed to sit in a container and checked for separation

_____ Other (describe) _____

_____

_____ **3.** Describe the results of the brake fluid contamination test. _____

_____

_____

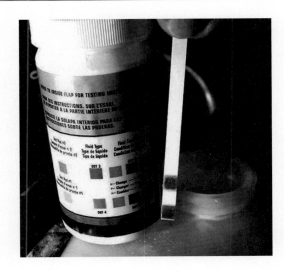

141

Manual Brake Bleeding

Meets NATEF Task: (A5-B-6) Bleed and/or flush brake system. (P-1)

Name _____ Date _____

Make/Model _____ Year _____ Instructor's OK [   ]

_____ **1.** Check the service information for the specified brake bleeding and flushing procedure for the vehicle being serviced. _____
_____

_____ **2.** Fill the master cylinder reservoir with clean brake fluid from a sealed container.

_____ **3.** Hoist the vehicle safely.

_____ **4.** Open the right rear bleeder valve and have an assistant slowly depress the brake pedal to bleed the wheel cylinder/caliper. Close the bleeder valve and have the assistant slowly release force on the brake pedal. Wait 15 seconds and repeat the process until a solid stream of brake fluid is observed.

_____ **5.** Repeat the bleeding procedures for the left-rear, right-front, and then the left-front wheel brakes.

_____ **6.** After all four wheel brakes have been bled, lower the vehicle and fill the master cylinder to the full mark.

> **CAUTION:** Check the master cylinder reservoir frequently and refill as necessary with clean brake fluid. Do not overfill a master cylinder reservoir.

_____ **7.** Test drive the vehicle checking for proper brake operation before returning the vehicle to the customer.

142

Pressure Brake Bleeding

Meets NATEF Task: (A5-B-6) Bleed and/or flush brake system. (P-1)

Name _____ Date _____

Make/Model _____ Year _____ Instructor's OK [ ]

_____ **1.** Check the service information for the specified brake bleeding procedure and sequence for the vehicle being serviced. Describe the specified procedure and sequence. _____

_____

_____ **2.** Fill the master cylinder reservoir with clean brake fluid from a sealed container.

_____ **3.** Hoist the vehicle safely.

_____ **4.** Open the right rear bleeder valve and use a pressure bleeder attached to the master cylinder using the correct adapter(s) to bleed the wheel cylinder/caliper until a solid stream of brake fluid is observed.

_____ **5.** Repeat the bleeding procedures for the left-rear, right-front, and then the left-front wheel brakes.

_____ **6.** After all four wheel brakes have been bled, lower the vehicle and fill the master cylinder to the full mark.

> **CAUTION:** Check the master cylinder reservoir frequently and refill as necessary with clean brake fluid. Do not overfill a master cylinder reservoir.

_____ **7.** Test drive the vehicle checking for proper brake operation before returning the vehicle to the customer.

143

Vacuum Brake Bleeding

Meets NATEF Task: (A5-B-6) Bleed and/or flush the brake system. (P-1)

Name _____ Date _____

Make/Model _____ Year _____ Instructor's OK [ ]

_____ 1. Check the service information for the specified brake bleeding procedure and sequence for the vehicle being serviced. Describe the procedure and bleeding sequence specified. _____

_____

_____ 2. Fill the master cylinder reservoir with clean brake fluid from a sealed container.

_____ 3. Hoist the vehicle safely.

_____ 4. Open the right rear bleeder valve and use a hand-operated or air-operated vacuum bleeder to bleed the wheel cylinder/caliper until a solid stream of brake fluid is observed.

_____ 5. Repeat the bleeding procedures for the other wheel brakes, usually left-rear, right-front, and then the left-front wheel brakes.

_____ 6. After all four wheel brakes have been bled, lower the vehicle and fill the master cylinder to the full mark.

> **CAUTION:** Check the master cylinder reservoir frequently and refill as necessary with clean brake fluid. Do not overfill a master cylinder reservoir.

_____ 7. Test drive the vehicle checking for proper brake operation before returning the vehicle to the customer.

144

Gravity Brake Bleeding

Meets NATEF Task: (A5-B-6) Bleed and/or flush the brake system. (P-1)

Name _____ Date _____

Make/Model _____ Year _____ Instructor's OK [ ]

_____ 1. Check the service information for the specified brake bleeding procedure and sequence for the vehicle being serviced. Describe the specified procedure and sequence. _____

_____

_____ 2. Fill the master cylinder reservoir with clean brake fluid from a sealed container.

_____ 3. Hoist the vehicle safely.

_____ 4. Open the right rear bleeder valve and wait until about a drip-per-second of brake fluid is observed coming out of the bleeder valve and close the bleeder valve.

_____ 5. Repeat the bleeding procedures for the left-rear, right-front, and then the left-front wheel brakes.

_____ 6. After all four wheel brakes have been bled, lower the vehicle and fill the master cylinder to the full mark.

CAUTION: Check the master cylinder reservoir frequently and refill as necessary with clean brake fluid. Do not overfill a master cylinder reservoir.

_____ 7. Test drive the vehicle checking for proper brake operation before returning the vehicle to the customer.

145

Brake Fluid Flush and Fill

Meets NATEF Task: (A5-B-6) Bleed and/or flush brake system. (P-1)

_____

Name _____ Date _____

Make/Model _____ Year _____ Instructor's OK [＿＿＿]

Many vehicle manufacturers recommend the replacement of brake fluid every 2 or 3 years (24,000 - 36,000 miles or 38,000 - 58,000 km).

_____ **1.** Check the service information for the specified brake bleeding procedure for the vehicle being serviced.

　　　　　 _____

　　　　　 _____

_____ **2.** Use a turkey baster or similar tool to remove most of the old brake fluid from the master cylinder reservoir.

_____ **3.** Refill the master cylinder with new brake fluid from a sealed container.

_____ **4.** Hoist the vehicle safely.

_____ **5.** Bleed the brake fluid from the right rear wheel brake until clean brake fluid is observed.

_____ **6.** Repeat the bleeding process for the left rear, right front, then the left front wheel brakes.

　　　　　 NOTE: Check the level of the brake fluid often and refill as necessary. Do not allow the master cylinder reservoir to become empty.

_____ **7.** After all the wheel brakes have been bled with clean brake fluid, lower the vehicle and test drive checking for proper operation of the brakes before returning the vehicle to the customer.

146

Wheel Bearing Service

Meets NATEF Task: (A5-F-1) Remove, clean, inspect, repack, and install wheel bearings and replace seals; install hub and adjust bearings. (P-1)

Name _____ Date _____

Make/Model _____ Year _____ Instructor's OK [____]

_____ **1.** Remove the wheel cover and the hub dust cap (grease cap).

_____ **2.** Remove and discard the cotter key.

_____ **3.** Remove the spindle nut, washer and outer bearing.

_____ **4.** Remove inner and outer bearing and grease seal.

_____ **5.** Thoroughly clean the bearing in solvent and denatured alcohol or brake cleaner and blow it dry with compressed air.

_____ **6.** Closely inspect the bearing for wear or damage.

_____ **7.** Show the instructor the cleaned bearing.   **Instructor's OK** _____

_____ **8.** Repack the bearing with the correct type of wheel bearing grease.

_____ **9.** Install a new grease seal using a seal installing tool.

_____ **10.** Correctly adjust the bearing preload:

> _____ Install the spindle nut and while rotating the tire assembly, tighten (snug only, 12 to 30 lb.-ft.) with a wrench to "seat" the bearing correctly in the race.
> _____ While still rotating the tire assembly, loosen the nut approximately 1/2 turn and then *hand tighten only*.
> _____ Install a new cotter key (the common size is 1/8" diameter and 1.5 inches long).
> _____ Bend the ends of the cotter key up and around the nut to prevent interference with the dust cap.

_____ **11.** Install the hub dust cap (grease cap) and wheel cover.

147

Wheel Bearing and Race Replacement

Meets NATEF Task: (A5-F-5) Replace wheel bearing and race. (P-2)

Name _____ Date_____

Make/Model _____ Year _____ Instructor's OK [ ]

_____ **1.** Remove the wheel cover and the hub dust cap (grease cap).

_____ **2.** Remove and discard the cotter key.

_____ **3.** Remove the spindle nut, washer and outer bearing.

_____ **4.** Remove inner and outer bearing and grease seal.

_____ **5.** Remove the bearing race using the specified tool.

_____ **6.** Show the instructor the removed race.
Instructor's OK _____

_____ **7.** Install new race using the correct bearing race installation tool.

_____ **8.** Show the instructor the new race.   **Instructor's OK** _____

_____ **9.** Install a new grease seal using a seal installing tool.

_____ **10.** Pack the new bearing with the correct type of wheel bearing grease.

_____ **11.** Correctly adjust the bearing preload:

_____ Install the spindle nut and while rotating the tire assembly, tighten (snug only, 12 to 30 lb.-ft.) with a wrench to "seat" the bearing correctly in the race.

_____ While still rotating the tire assembly, loosen the nut approximately 1/2 turn and then *hand tighten only*.

_____ Install a new cotter key (the common size is 1/8" diameter and 1.5 inches long).

_____ Bend the ends of the cotter key up and around the nut to prevent interference with the dust cap.

_____ **12.** Install the hub dust cap (grease cap) and wheel cover.

148

Drum Brake Service

Meets NATEF Task: (A5-C-3) Remove, clean, inspect drum brake parts; determine necessary action. (P-1)

Name _____ Date _____

Make/Model _____ Year _____ Instructor's OK [ ]

_____ 1. Hoist the vehicle safely to a good working height (about chest high).

_____ 2. Remove the rear wheels on a vehicle equipped with rear drum brakes.

_____ 3. Remove the brake drums (they should pull straight off - if you have problems, see the instructor).

_____ 4. Check the thickness of the brake lining remaining.

   OK _____   NOT OK _____   Describe any faults _____

_____ 5. Remove the old brake shoes and hardware.

_____ 6. Clean, inspect, and lubricate the backing plate.

_____ 7. Clean and lubricate the star-wheel adjuster.

Lubricate washers
and socket pivot

Lubricate threads

_____ 8. Check or replace all hardware including the hold-down springs and return springs.

_____ 9. Install the brake shoes, hardware, springs, and self adjuster.

_____10. Adjust the brake shoes using a drum-shoe clearance gauge.

149

Wheel Cylinder Inspection and Replacement

Meets NATEF Task: (A5-C-4) Inspect and install wheel cylinders. (P-2)

Name _____ Date _____

Make/Model _____ Year _____ Instructor's OK [ ]

_____ 1. Check the service information for the specified procedure for wheel cylinder replacement for the vehicle being serviced. _____

_____ 2. Hoist the vehicle safely and remove the rear wheels and brake drums.

_____ 3. Use a dull tool and lift the edge of the dust boots on the wheel cylinder.

      _____ Brake fluid dripped out (requires overhaul or replacement)

      _____ Dust boot is wet (normal, further inspection may be needed)

      _____ Dust boot is dry (normal, further inspection may be needed)

_____ 4. Remove the brake shoes to allow access to the wheel cylinders.

> **HINT:** Some service technicians apply the parking brake to force the brake shoe away from the wheel cylinder providing the clearance necessary to remove or replace the wheel cylinder without having to remove the brake shoe.

_____ 5. Remove the wheel cylinder from the backing plate and disassemble.

_____ 6. Reinstall the wheel cylinder, brake linings, drums, and bleed the system.

_____ 7. Lower the vehicle and test the brakes for proper operation.

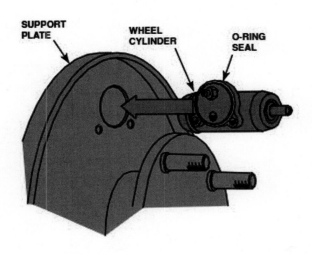

150

Pre-Adjustment of Brake Shoes

Meets NATEF Task: (A5-C-5) Pre-adjust brake shoes and parking brake; install brake drums or drum/hub assemblies and wheel bearings. (P-2)

Name _____ Date _____

Make/Model _____ Year _____ Instructor's OK [ ]

Brake shoes should be pre-adjusted close to the working clearance between the brake shoes and the brake drum before the brake drum is installed.

_____ 1. Assemble the drum brake and verify that all parts are properly lubricated.

_____ 2. Using a brake shoe clearance gauge, insert it into the drum and turn the lock knob to hold the setting.

SHOE SETTING CALIPER LOCK SCREW

_____ 3. Install the brake shoe clearance gauge over the brake shoes and turn the adjuster until the lining contacts the gauge.

SHOE SETTING CALIPER

_____ 4. Verify the pre-adjustment by installing the drum. It should slide over the brake shoes with little clearance.

OK _____   NOT OK _____

151

Install Wheel and Torque Lug Nuts

Meets NATEF Task: (A5-C-6) Install wheel and torque lug nuts and make final checks and adjustments. (P-1)

Name _____ Date _____

Make/Model _____ Year _____ Instructor's OK [ ]

_____ **1.** Check service information and determine the vehicle manufacturer's specified lug nut torque specification.

_____ (usually between 80 and 100 lb-ft)

_____ **2.** Use a hand-operated wire brush on the wheel studs to ensure clean and dry threads and check for damage.

OK _____ **NOT OK** _____ Describe fault: _____

_____ **3.** Verify that the lug nuts are OK and free of defects.

_____ **4.** Install the wheel over the studs and start all lug nuts (or bolts) by hand.

_____ **5.** Tighten the lug nuts a little at a time in a star pattern using an air impact wrench equipped with the proper torque limiting adapter or a torque wrench.

_____ Used a torque wrench

_____ Used an air impact with a torque limiting adapter (torque stick)

_____ **6.** Tighten the lug nuts to final torque in a star pattern.

NOTE: "Tighten one, skip one, tighten one" is the usual method if four or five lug nuts are used.

152

Disc Brake Caliper Inspection

Meets NATEF Task: (A5-D-1) Remove caliper assembly, inspect for leaks and damage to caliper housing; determine necessary action. (P-1)

Name _____ Date _____

Make/Model _____ Year _____ Instructor's OK [   ]

_____ **1.** Hoist the vehicle safely and remove the front wheels.

_____ **2.** Loosen the bleeder valve and push the caliper piston into the caliper.

_____ **3.** Remove the caliper and pads.

_____ **4.** Check the caliper mountings for damage or wear.

_____ **5.** Check for brake fluid leaks and cracked

           flex hoses.

             OK ____   NOT OK ____

_____ **6.** Based on the inspection results, what is the necessary action?

_____

_____

153

Caliper Mounting and Slide

Meets NATEF Task: (A5-D-2) Clean and inspect caliper mounting and slides/pins for operation, wear, and damage; determine necessary action. (P-1)

Name _____ Date _____

Make/Model _____ Year _____ Instructor's OK ☐

_____ 1. Check service information for the specified cleaning and measurements for caliper slides and/or mounting points.

_____

_____

_____ 2. Remove the calipers from the steering knuckle assembly and describe the type of mounting (check all that apply):

____ Sliding-type caliper
____ Guide pin-mounted caliper
____ Fixed caliper

_____ 3. Inspect the mounting and slides for wear (describe):

_____

_____

_____

_____

OK ____ **NOT OK** ____

_____ 4. Based on the inspection and the vehicle manufacturer's recommended procedures, what is the necessary action?

_____

_____

154

Remove and Inspect Disc Brake Pads

Meets NATEF Task: (A5-D-3) Remove, inspect, and replace pads and retaining hardware; determine necessary action. (P-1)

Name _____ **Date** _____

Make/Model _____ **Year** _____ **Instructor's OK** [　　]

_____ **1.** Check the service information for the specified procedure for removing and reinstalling disc brake pads. _____

_____

_____

_____ **2.** The procedure usually includes the following steps.

    A. Hoist the vehicle safely to a good working height.

    B. Remove the wheels.

    C. Remove the caliper retaining bolts and slide the caliper assembly off of the rotor.

> **NOTE:** The caliper piston may need to be pushed into the caliper to provide the necessary clearance to remove the caliper from the rotor. Most vehicle manufacturers recommend that the bleeder valve be opened before the caliper piston is pushed inward to prevent brake fluid from being forced backward into the ABS hydraulic unit or master cylinder.

_____ **3.** Remove the pads from the caliper and inspect them for wear, cracks, and chips.

    OK _____ **NOT OK** _____

_____ **4.** Measure pad thickness and compare to the specification. Measured thickness of friction material = _____. Minimum allowable = _____.

_____ **5.** Based on the inspection, what is the necessary action?

_____

_____

155

Disc Brake Caliper Assembly

Meets NATEF Task: (A5-D-4) Lubricate and reinstall caliper, pads, and related hardware; seat pads and inspect for leaks. (P-1)

Name _____ Date _____

Make/Model _____ Year _____ Instructor's OK [____]

_____ **1.** Check the service information for the specified procedure to follow for the lubrication and installation of caliper and pad. _____

_____

_____ **2.** Lubricate the specified slides. Describe the location. _____

_____

_____ **3.** Install caliper and pads and torque fasteners to factory specifications.
Specified torque = _____

_____ **4.** Seat the pads.

_____ **5.** After installation of the caliper and pads, bleed the system.

_____ **6.** Check for leaks and proper operation.

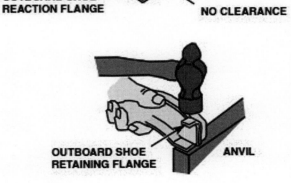

156

Brake Pad Wear Indicator System

Meets NATEF Task: (A5-D-10) Check brake pad wear indicator system operation; determine necessary action. (P-2)

Name _____ Date _____

Make/Model _____ Year _____ Instructor's OK [ ]

_____ 1. Check service information for the specified procedure to follow when checking the brake pad wear indicator system. Describe specified instructions: _____

_____

_____

_____ 2. What type of brake pad wear indicates that the system was tested? (check all that apply)

     _____ **Wear sensor on pads** (makes noise when pads are worn)

     _____ **Dash warning lamp** (triggered by the sensor in the brake)

     _____ **Slits cut in the disc brake pads** that indicate minimum allowable thickness

_____ 3. Based on the inspection of the brake pad wear indicator system, what is the necessary action?

_____

157

Remove and Replace a Disc Brake Rotor

Meets NATEF Task: (A5-D-6) Remove and reinstall rotor. (P-1)

Name _____ Date _____

Make/Model _____ Year _____ Instructor's OK ☐

_____ **1.** Hoist the vehicle safely and remove the wheels.

_____ **2.** Wet the disc brake caliper and pads or install a vacuum enclosure to provide protection against possible asbestos dust.

_____ **3.** Remove the caliper retaining fasteners and remove the caliper assembly.

_____ **4.** Use a stiff wire and support the caliper.

> **CAUTION:** Do not allow the caliper to hang by the flexible brake hose.

_____ **5.** Remove the disc brake rotor.

    A. If a hub-type rotor, remove the dust cover, cotter pins, retaining nut, and remove the bearings and rotor from the spindle.
    B. If a hubless rotor, remove the rotor from the hub.

_____ **6.** Clean the rotor contact surfaces.

_____ **7.** Reinstall the rotor. If a hub-type rotor, adjust the wheel bearing according to manufacturer's specifications.

_____ **8.** Reinstall the caliper assembly.

_____ **9.** Depress the brake pedal several times to restore proper braking action.

_____ **10.** Reinstall the wheels, torque the lug nuts to factory specifications, and lower the vehicle.

158

Brake Pad Break-In Procedure

Meets NATEF Task: (A5-D-11) Describe the importance of performing proper burnish/break-in of replacement brake pads. (P-1)

Name _____ Date _____

Make/Model _____ Year _____ Instructor's OK [   ]

_____ 1. Check service information for the exact procedure to follow to properly burnish/break-in replacement brake pads. Describe specified procedures. _____

_____

_____

_____

_____ 2. Check service information and describe the importance of why replacement brake pads should be burnished/broken-in. _____

_____

_____

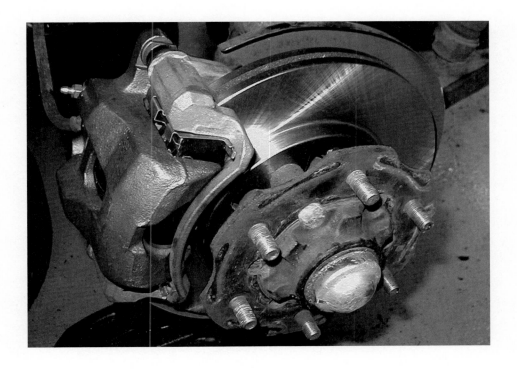

159

Disc Brake Integral Parking Brake Service

Meets NATEF Task: (A5-D-9) Retract and re-adjust caliper piston on an integral parking brake system. (P-3)

Name _____ **Date** _____

Make/Model _____ **Year** _____ **Instructor's OK** ☐

_____ 1. Check service information for the specified procedure to follow when retracting and re-adjusting the caliper piston on an integral parking brake system. Describe the specified procedure. _____

_____

_____

_____ 2. Check all that apply.

_____ Required specific steps

_____ Required a gauge

_____ Required a special tool

_____ Other (describe) _____

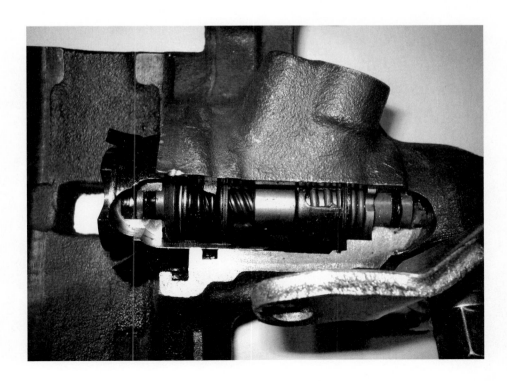

160

Parking Brake Adjustment

Meets NATEF Task: (A5-F-2) Check parking brake cables and components for wear and clean, lubricate, adjust or replace as necessary (P-2)

Name _____ Date _____

Make/Model _____ Year _____ Instructor's OK [ ]

_____ 1. Check the service information for the specified parking brake lubrication and

adjustment for the vehicle being serviced. _____

_____ 2. Apply the parking brake and count the number of "clicks."

_____ less than 4 "clicks"
_____ 5 - 10 "clicks"
_____ over 10 "clicks"

NOTE: If there are less than 4 "clicks" or more than 10 "clicks", adjustment of the parking brake may be necessary.

_____ 3. Place the gear selector in neutral and release the parking brake.

_____ 4. Hoist the vehicle safely.

_____ 5. Try rotating the rear wheels (front wheels on some Subaru vehicles).

_____ rotates freely   _____ does not rotate

NOTE: If the rear wheels do not rotate, try loosening the parking brake cable.

_____ 6. If the rear wheels rotate freely and the parking brake requires more than 10 "clicks,"

remove the rear brakes for inspection.

NOTE: The parking brake should only be adjusted after checking and adjusting the rear brakes.

_____ 7. Clean and adjust the rear brakes.

_____ 8. Reassemble the rear brakes and apply the parking brake 3 - 4 "clicks."

_____ 9. If the rear wheels can be rotated, adjust the parking

brake adjuster until the rear wheel brakes are just

touching the brake drums.

_____ 10. Apply the parking brake and again count the

"clicks." Most vehicle manufacturers recommend

that the parking brake should hold with 6 to 18

"clicks." Readjust the parking brake as necessary.

161

Parking Brake Indicator Light

Meets NATEF Task: (A5-F-3) Check parking brake operation and parking brake indicator light system operation; determine necessary action. (P-1)

Name _____ Date _____

Make/Model _____ Year _____ Instructor's OK [   ]

A dash warning lamp should light whenever the parking brake is applied when the ignition is on. To verify that the parking brake indicator light functions correctly, follow these steps.

_____ 1. Turn the ignition to on (run).

> **NOTE:** The engine can be started to be sure that the ignition is on.

_____ 2. Apply the parking brake (check one of the following).

    ____ Hand-operated lever
    ____ Foot-operated pedal
    ____ Push button-operated parking brake

_____ 3. Did the red brake warning light come on?

    ____ Yes   ____ No

_____ 4. Check service information for the recommended procedures to follow if the parking brake indicator lamp did not work correctly.

_____

_____ 5. Based on the inspection, what is the necessary action? _____

_____

162

Brake Drum Measurement

Meets NATEF Task: (A5-C-1) Remove, clean, inspect, and measure brake drums; determine necessary action. (P-1)

Name _____ Date _____

Make/Model _____ Year _____ Instructor's OK ☐

_____ **1.** Wet the brake drum or use an enclosure to help
protect against asbestos exposure.

_____ **2.** Remove the brake drum from the vehicle and
label the left and right to ensure that the
drum is replaced in the original location.

_____ **3.** Thoroughly inspect the brake drum.

- Hot (hard) spots

    OK_____ **NOT OK**_____ (requires replacement)

- Tap with a hammer. The brake drum should ring like a bell if not cracked.

    OK_____ **NOT OK**_____ (requires replacement)

_____ **4.** Determine the maximum allowable inside diameter of the brake drum or the
maximum "turn to" dimension.

Maximum allowable inside diameter = _____ (allow 0.030" for wear)

Maximum "turn to" diameter = _____

_____ **5.** Measure the drum using a drum micrometer.

Left = _____   Right = _____

OK to machine _____   **NOT OK to machine** _____

_____ **6.** Based on the inspection, what is the necessary action? _____

_____

163

Machining a Brake Drum

Meets NATEF Task: (A5-C-2) Refinish brake drum; measure final drum diameter. (P-1)

Name _____ **Date** _____

Make/Model _____ **Year** _____ **Instructor's OK** ☐

_____ 1. Measure the drum and double check that the brake drum can be safely machined.

      • Maximum allowable inside diameter = _____
      • Actual measurement of the drum = _____ left = _____ right = _____

      OK to machine _____   **discard** _____

_____ 2. Select the proper tapered centering cone and face supporting plate.

_____ 3. Install a self-aligning spacer (SAS) and tighten the spindle nut.

_____ 4. Perform a scratch cut.

_____ 5. Stop the lathe, loosen the spindle nut, and rotate the brake drum 180° (one-half turn) and retighten the spindle nut.

_____ 6. Perform a second scratch cut.

      • If the second cut is in the same location, proceed with machining.
      • If the second cut is on the opposite side of the drum, clean or repair the lathe before machining.

_____ 7. Install a silencer band (vibration damper).

_____ 8. Machine the drum.

_____ 9. The measurement of the drum after machining = _____.

      Does this allow 0.030" or more for wear?

      Yes ____ (install on the vehicle)   **No** ____ (replace the drum)

164

Brake Rotor Measurement

Meets NATEF Task: (A5-D-5)Clean, inspect, and measure rotor thickness, lateral runout, and thickness variation; determine necessary action. (P-1)

Name _____ Date _____

Make/Model _____ Year _____ Instructor's OK [ ]

_____ **1.** Visually inspect the brake rotor for:

- hard spots **OK** ____ **NOT OK** ____ (requires replacement)
- excessive rust **OK** ____ **NOT OK** ____
- deep grooves (over 0.060" deep) **OK** ____ **NOT OK** ____

_____ **2.** Check the service information and determine the specifications and measurements for thickness.

Minimum thickness = _____

Machine-to-thickness = _____

Actual thickness = _____ **OK** ____ **NOT OK** ____

_____ **3.** Determine the specifications for thickness variation (parallelism).

_____

_____ **4.** Using a micrometer, measure the thickness at four or more locations around the rotor to determine the thickness variation (parallelism). (Usually 0.0005" or less difference in the readings.)

A. _____   C. _____   E. _____

B. _____   D. _____   F.

_____

OK ____   **NOT OK** ____

_____ **5.** Use a dial indicator and measure the runout of the rotor.

Runout = _____ (should be less than 0.005 in.)

OK ____   **NOT OK** ____

_____ **6.** Based on the measurements and manufacturer's recommendations, should the rotor be replaced or machined? Why? _____

_____

165

On-the-Vehicle Lathe

Meets NATEF Task: (A5-D-7) Refinish rotor on the vehicle; measure final rotor thickness.
(P-1)

Name _____ Date _____

Make/Model _____ Year _____ Instructor's OK [____]

_____ 1. Hoist the vehicle safely to the proper height according to the lathe manufacturer's instructions and remove the front wheels.

_____ 2. Mount the on-the-vehicle lathe according to the lathe manufacturer's instructions and calibrate the lathe as necessary.

> **NOTE:** On caliper mounted on-the-vehicle lathe, the disc brake caliper must be removed and supported with a wire to help prevent damage to the hydraulic flexible brake line.

_____ 3. Machine the rotor following the lathe manufacturer's instructions.

_____ 4. Use 150 grit aluminum oxide sandpaper on a block or a grinding disc to provide the required smooth non-directional finish.

_____ 5. Thoroughly clean both disc brake rotors before installing the replacement disc brake pads and reinstalling the disc brake caliper.

> **NOTE:** Be sure to install all anti-noise shims and hardware.

_____ 6. Reinstall the front wheels and tighten the lug nuts to factory specifications in a star pattern (tighten one, skip one, etc.) using a torque wrench on a torque-limiting adjuster with an air impact wrench.

_____ 7. Lower the vehicle and depress the brake pedal several times to achieve proper brake pedal height.

_____ 8. Test drive the vehicle before returning the vehicle to the customer.

On-the-Vehicle Lathe

166

Machining a Brake Rotor Off Vehicle

Meets NATEF Task: (A5-D-8) Refinish rotor off the vehicle; measure final rotor thickness.
(P-1)

Name _____ Date _____

Make/Model _____ Year _____ Instructor's OK [ ]

_____ **1.** Carefully inspect the rotor for hot spots or damage.

> **OK** _____ **NOT OK** _____ (requires replacement of the rotor)

_____ **2.** Determine minimum rotor thickness = _____ or machine to thickness = _____

_____ **3.** Measure the rotor thickness = _____. **OK to machine___ NOT OK to machine___**

_____ **4.** Clean the brake lathe spindle.

_____ **5.** Select the proper tapered cover and/or collets to properly secure the rotor to the lathe spindle.

_____ **6.** Install the self-aligning spacer (SAS) and tighten the spindle nut.

_____ **7.** Install the silencer band (noise damper).

_____ **8.** Perform a scratch test.

_____ **9.** Stop the lathe and loosen the spindle nut.

_____ **10.** Rotate the rotor 180° (one-half turn) and tighten the spindle nut.

_____ **11.** Perform another scratch cut. If the second scratch cut is in the same location as the first scratch cut or extends completely around the rotor, the machining of the rotor can continue. (If the second scratch cut is 180 from the first scratch cut, remove the rotor and clean the spindle and attaching hardware. Repeat the scratch test.)

_____ **12.** Machine the rotor removing as little material as possible.

_____ **13.** Measure the rotor with a micrometer to be sure rotor thickness is still within limits.

_____ **14.** Use 150 grit aluminum oxide sandpaper on a block of wood for 60 seconds on each side or a grinder to provide a smooth non-directional finish.

_____ **15.** Thoroughly clean the rotor friction surface.

_____ **16.** Remove the rotor from the lathe.

167

Power Brake Booster Test

Meets NATEF Task: (A5-E-1) Test pedal free travel; check power assist operation.
(P-2)

Name _____ Date _____

Make/Model _____ Year _____ Instructor's OK [ ]

_____ 1. Check the service information for the specified procedure for testing a vacuum power brake booster for the vehicle being serviced.

_____

_____ 2. With the engine off, depress the brake pedal several times until the brake pedal feels hard (firm).

_____ 3. The brake pedal should not fall to the floor of the vehicle.

OK _____   NOT OK _____

_____ 4. With your foot still firmly depressing the brake pedal, start the engine. The brake pedal should go down.

OK _____   NOT OK _____

← Forward   Rearward →

Diaphragm hub

Atmospheric chamber

Valve housing

Master cylinder push rod

Filter

Operating rod

Reaction disc

Poppet assembly

Valve plunger

Check valve   Vacuum chamber

Diaphragm

168

Vacuum Supply/Manifold or Auxiliary Pump

Meets NATEF Task: (A5-E-2) Check vacuum supply to vacuum-type power booster.
(P-2)

Name _____ Date _____

Make/Model _____ Year _____ Instructor's OK [ ]

_____ 1. Check service information for the recommended procedures and specifications for checking vacuum supply to power booster.

_____

_____

_____

_____ 2. Is the vehicle equipped with an auxiliary vacuum pump? _____ Yes _____ No

_____ 3. Most vehicle manufacturers specify that a vacuum "T" be installed in the vacuum line between the intake manifold and/or auxiliary pump and the vacuum power brake booster assembly. Most manufacturers specify a minimum of 15 in. Hg. of vacuum be measured.

Actual vacuum measured at the power brake booster = _____

____ OK ____ NOT OK

169

Inspect the Hydraulic Clutch

Meets NATEF Task: (A3-B-1and A3-B-2) Inspect hydraulic clutch slave and master cylinders; determine necessary action. (P-1)

Name _____ Date _____

Make/Model _____ Year _____ Instructor's OK [ ]

_____ 1. Check service information and determine the specified test procedures to follow when inspecting the hydraulic clutch linkage system for proper operation (describe procedures).

_____

_____

_____

_____ 2. If there is any sign of fluid leakage, describe the location. _____

_____

_____

_____ 3. Based on the inspection, what is the necessary action? _____

_____

_____

170

Check Manual Transmission/Transaxle Fluid

Meets NATEF Task: (A3-A-3) Check fluid condition; check for leaks. (P-2)

Name _____ **Date** _____

Make/Model _____ **Year** _____ **Instructor's OK** [   ]

_____ **1.** Check the service manual for correct fluid and for the location for inspecting the fluid.

             Recommended fluid _____

             Inspection location (describe) _____

_____ **2.** Inspect the fluid level.

             _____ Level okay
             _____ Level low - added fluid

_____ **3.** Describe the condition of the fluid (color, smell, etc.) _____

_____

_____ **4.** Check for leaks.

             _____ **OK**   _____ **NOT OK**

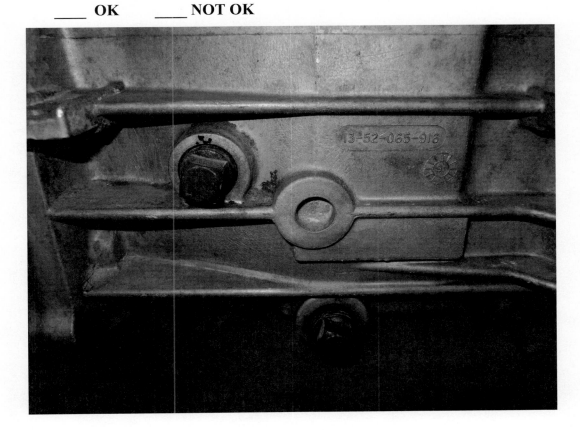

171

Drain and Fill Manual Transmission/Transaxle

Meets NATEF Task: (A3-A-2) Drain and refill manual transmission/transaxle and final drive unit. (P-1)

Name _____ Date _____

Make/Model _____ Year _____ Instructor's OK [ ]

Use service information to determine the following information.

_____ 1. List the brand name and designation of the manual transmission/transaxle.

      Brand name _____ Designation _____

_____ 2. List the specified lubricant and the capacity.

      Lubricant _____ Capacity _____

_____ 3. Drain manual transmission/transaxle fluid. Dispose of all fluid according to Federal

      State, and local laws.

_____ 4. Refill manual transmission/transaxle and final drive unit.

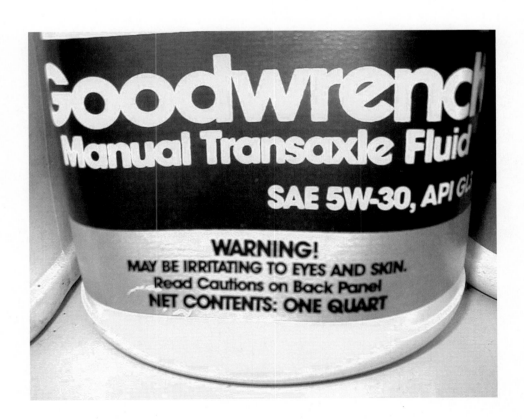

172

Front Wheel Drive Bearings and Hubs

Meets NATEF Task: (A3-D-1) Inspect, remove, and replace front wheel drive bearings, hubs, and seals. (P-2)

Name _____ **Date** _____

Make/Model _____ **Year** _____ **Instructor's OK** [ ]

_____ 1. Check service information for the specified procedure to follow when inspecting and replacing a front wheel drive bearing, hub, and seal. Describe specified procedures.

_____

_____

_____ 2. What was the specified torque of the fasteners?

- Axle nut _____

- Strut mount (if applicable) _____

- Other (describe) _____

_____ 3. Remove front wheel drive bearing, hub, and seal.

_____ 4. Inspect bearing, hub, and seal and describe the condition. _____

_____

_____

_____ 5. Install front wheel drive bearing, hub, and seals; torque all fasteners to factory specifications.

173

Service Drive Shafts and Joints

Meets NATEF Task: (A3-D-2) Inspect, service, and replace shafts, yokes, boots, and universal/CV joints. (P-2)

Name _____ Date _____

Make/Model _____ Year _____ Instructor's OK ☐

_____ 1. Check service information for the specified procedure to follow when replacing drive shafts and joints. Describe the specified procedure for the vehicle being serviced.

_____

_____

_____

_____ 2. Check all that apply.

　　　_____ Rear-wheel-drive vehicle

　　　_____ Front-wheel-drive vehicle

　　　_____ All-wheel-drive vehicle

　　　_____ CV joints inspected/replaced

　　　_____ V-joints inspected/replaced

_____ 3. Remove drive shaft.　　**Instructor's OK** _____

_____ 4. Replace universal/CV joint/boots.　　**Instructor's OK** _____

_____ 5. What fault(s) was discovered during the inspection? Describe. _____

_____

_____ 6. Install drive shaft.

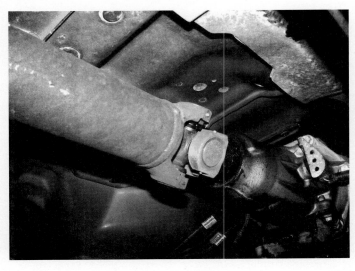

174

Differential Assembly Service

Meets NATEF Task: (A3-E-1, A3-E-2, A3-E-3) Inspect differential housing for leaks; check vent; check level and drain and refill assembly. (P-1)

___

Name _____ **Date** _____

Make/Model _____ **Year** _____ **Instructor's OK** [____]

_____ 1. Check service information for the specified fluid to use in the differential housing assembly. _____

_____

_____ 2. Check the differential fluid level.

_____ **OK** _____ **NOT OK**

_____ 3. Check vent. _____ **OK** _____ **NOT OK**

_____ 4. Check the differential housing for leaks.

_____ **OK** _____ **NOT OK**

_____ 5. Drain and refill the differential housing.

- Quantity of fluid required _____
- SAE grade used _____
- Limited-slip additive needed? _____

175

Inspect and Replace Drive Axle Wheel Studs

Meets NATEF Task: (A3-F-1) Inspect and replace drive axle wheel studs. (P-2)

Name _____ Date _____

Make/Model _____ Year _____ Instructor's OK [ ]

_____ **1.** Check service information for the specified procedure to follow when replacing the
wheel studs on a drive axle. Describe the specified procedure. _____

_____

_____

_____ **2.** List the tools needed.

_____   _____

_____   _____

_____   _____

_____ **3.** What is the specified wheel lug nut torque? _____

Inspect and Replace Drive Axle Wheel Studs

Meets NATEF Task: (A4-F-11) Inspect and replace drive axle wheel studs. (P-2)

Name _____ Date _____

Make/Model _____ Year _____ Instructor's OK ☐

1. Check service information for the specified procedure to follow when replacing the wheel studs on a drive axle. Describe the specified procedure.

_____

2. List the tools needed.

_____

3. What is the specified wheel lug nut torque?

_____

176

Inspect Front Locking Hubs

Meets NATEF Task: (A3-G-1) Inspect front bearings and locking hubs; perform necessary action. (P-3)

Name _____ Date _____

Make/Model _____ Year _____ Instructor's OK [ ]

_____ 1. Check service information for the recommended procedures to follow when inspecting front bearings and locking hubs. Describe the inspection procedures. _____

_____

_____

_____

_____ 2. Based on the inspection, what is the necessary action? _____

_____

_____

_____

177

Transfer Case Lube Level Check

Meets NATEF Task: (A3-G-2) Check transfer case lube level and vents/seals.
(P-3)

Name _____ Date _____

Make/Model _____ Year _____ Instructor's OK [   ]

_____ **1.** Check service information for the specified methods to follow to check the seals, vents, and lube level (describe). _____

_____

_____

_____

_____ **2.** What is the specified lube? _____

_____ **3.** Were the vents clear? **Yes** _____ **No** _____ If no, describe why they were clogged.

_____

_____

_____ **4.** Were the seals okay? **Yes** _____ **No** _____ If no, describe which seals were leaking.

_____

_____

178

Describe Operation of a Continuously Variable Transmission

Meets NATEF Task: (A2-C-1) Describe the operation of a continuously variable transmission (CVT). (P-3)

Name _____ **Date** _____

Make/Model _____ **Year** _____ **Instructor's OK** [   ]

_____ **1.** Check service information and reference materials and describe the operation of a continuously variable transmission (CVT). Describe the operation. _____

_____

_____

_____ **2.** What is the specified fluid for the CVT unit in the vehicle being serviced? _____

_____

_____

- Type _____
- Viscosity _____
- Color _____
- Cost _____
- Amount required for service charge _____

Describe Operation of a Continuously Variable Transmission

Meets NATEF Task: (A2-E-1) Describe the operation of a continuously variable transmission (CVT) (P-3).

Name		Date		
Make/Model		Year		Instructor's OK

_____ 1. Check service information and reference material and describe the operation of a continuously variable transmission (CVT). First, list the operation. _____

_____ 2. What is the specified fluid for the CVT used in the vehicle being serviced?

a. Type _____

b. Viscosity _____

c. Color _____

d. Odor _____

e. Amount required for service change. _____

179

Describe the Operation of a Hybrid Vehicle Drive Train

Meets NATEF Task: (A2-C-2) Describe the operation of a hybrid vehicle drive train. (P-3)

Name _____ **Date** _____

Make/Model _____ **Year** _____ **Instructor's OK** ☐

_____ 1. Check service information and reference materials and describe the operating characteristics of a hybrid electric vehicle drive train. _____

_____

_____

_____

_____ 2. The type of hybrid electric vehicle studied uses (check all that apply):

_____ One motor system

_____ Two motor system

_____ Three motor system

_____ Modified conventional automatic transmission

_____ Hybrid unique transmission

_____ Rear-wheel drive

_____ Front-wheel Drive

_____ All-wheel drive

Describe the Operation of a Hybrid Vehicle Drive Train

Meets NATEF Task: (A3/6-E.2) Describe the operation of a hybrid drive train. (I.xx)

Name _____ Date _____

Make/Model _____ Year _____ Instructor's OK [ ]

1. Check prior information and reference materials and describe the operating principles of a hybrid electric vehicle drive train.

2. The type of hybrid electric vehicle studied uses (check all that apply):

   ___ Lubrication system
   ___ Two motor system
   ___ Three motor system
   ___ Modified conventional automatic transmission
   ___ Hybrid unique transmission
   ___ Rear axle battery
   ___ Front wheel drive
   ___ All wheel drive

180

Describe Operation of a Dual-Clutch Automatic

Meets NATEF Task: (A3-C-1) Describe the operation of an electronically-controlled manual transmission (transaxle). (P-3)

Name _____ Date _____

Make/Model _____ Year _____ Instructor's OK [   ]

_____ 1. Check service information and reference materials and describe the operating

characteristics of a dual-clutch automatic _____

_____

_____

_____

_____ 2. The type of dual-clutch transmission studied uses (check all that apply):

    _____ Dry clutch

    _____ Wet clutch

    _____ Number of forward speeds = _____

    _____ Specified fluid = _____

    _____ Specified service interval = _____

181

Check Fluid Level with a Dipstick

Meets NATEF Task: (A2-A-2) Check fluid level in a transmission/transaxle equipped with a dipstick. (P-1)

Name _____ Date _____

Make/Model _____ Year _____ Instructor's OK [   ]

_____ 1. Check service information for the specified procedure to follow when checking the fluid level in an automatic transmission/transaxle equipped with a dipstick. Describe the procedure. _____

_____

_____

_____ 2. The specified procedure requires which steps (check all that apply)?

_____ Normal operating temperature

_____ Gear selector in neutral (N)

_____ Gear selector in park (P)

_____ Vehicle on level ground

_____ Engine running

_____ Engine not running

_____ Other (describe) _____

_____ 3. Fluid level was: _____ **OK** _____ **NOT OK** Describe _____

_____

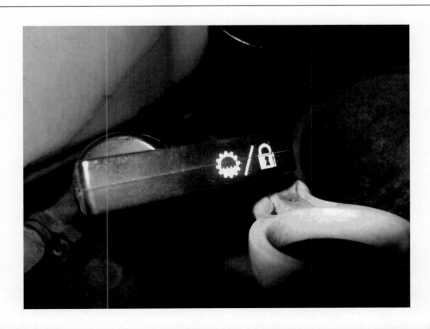

182

Check Fluid Level without a Dipstick

Meets NATEF Task: (A2-A-3) Check fluid level in a transmission/transaxle not equipped with a dipstick. (P-1)

Name _____ **Date** _____

Make/Model _____ **Year** _____ **Instructor's OK** ☐

_____ **1.** Check service information for the specified procedure to check an automatic transmission/transaxle not equipped with a dipstick. Describe the procedure.

_____

_____

_____ **2.** The specified procedure requires which steps (check all that apply)?

    _____ Use a scan tool to determine the specified fluid temperature

    _____ Gear selector in neutral (N)

    _____ Gear selector in park (P)

    _____ Vehicle on level ground

    _____ Engine running

    _____ Engine not running

    _____ Removal of an access plug

    _____ Other (describe) _____

_____

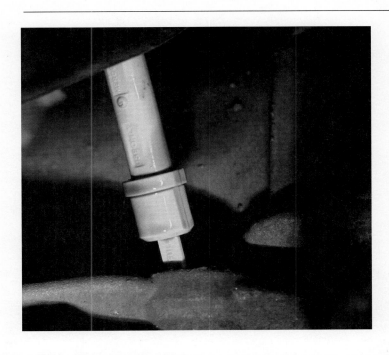

183

Check ATF Condition and Leaks

Meets NATEF Task: (A2-A-4 and A2-B-2) Check transmission fluid condition; check for leaks. (P-2)

Name _____ **Date** _____

Make/Model _____ **Year** _____ **Instructor's OK** [ ]

_____ 1. Check service information for the specified procedure to follow when checking fluid condition. Describe the specified procedure. _____

_____

_____ 2. Based on the inspection, what is the condition of the fluid? _____

_____

_____ 3. Check service information for the specified method to use to check for fluid leaks. Check all that apply.

_____ Engine running

_____ Dye/black light

_____ Powder

_____ Engine off

_____ Other (specify) _____

_____ 4. Based on the inspection, where is there a leak? Describe the location. _____

_____

_____

184

Inspect and Adjust External Linkage

Meets NATEF Task: (A2-B-1) Inspect and adjust external shift linkage and switch/sensor.
(P-2)

Name _____ **Date** _____

Make/Model _____ **Year** _____ **Instructor's OK** ☐

_____ 1. Check service information for the specified methods and procedures to follow to check and adjust the manual shift linkage and transmission range switch/sensor assembly. Describe specified procedures. _____

_____

_____

_____ 2. What tools/equipment are required to perform this adjustment. Check all that apply.

_____ Scan tool

_____ Hand tools

_____ DMM

_____ Other (describe) _____

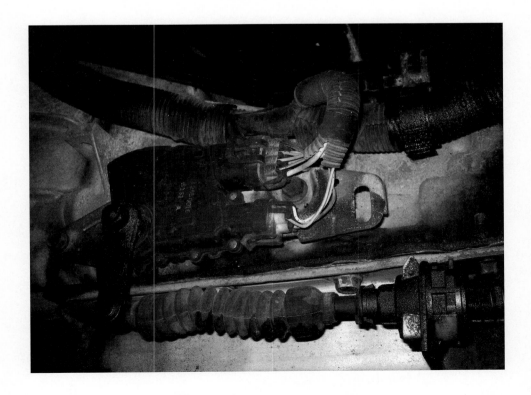

185

Inspect Power Train Mounts

Meets NATEF Task: (A2-B-3) Inspect power train mounts. (P-2)

Name _____ Date _____

Make/Model _____ Year _____ Instructor's OK [   ]

_____ 1. Check service information for the specified procedure to follow to inspect power train mounts. Describe procedures. _____

_____

_____

_____ 2. What tools and equipment were specified to be used? Check all that apply.

_____ Hoist

_____ Pry bar

_____ Hand tools

_____ Power tools

_____ Measuring rule

_____ Other (describe) _____

_____ 3. What was the condition of the power train mounts? Describe the condition.

_____

_____

Inspect Power Train Mounts

Meets NATEF Task: (A2.D.3) Inspect power train mounts. (P-2)

Name _____ Date _____

Make/model _____ Year _____ Instructor's OK [ ]

1. Locate correct information for the specified procedure to follow in manual. Describe the procedure.

2. What special equipment were the tools to be used? Check all that apply.
   - Hoist
   - Pry bar
   - Materials
   - Vacuum gauge
   - Measuring rule
   - Other (describe)

3. What was the condition of the power train mounts? Describe the condition.

186

Drain and Replace Fluid and Filter(s)

Meets NATEF Task: (A2-B-4) Drain and replace fluid and filter(s). (P-1)

Name _____ Date _____

Make/Model _____ Year _____ Instructor's OK [____]

_____ 1. Check service information for the specified procedure to follow to drain and replace the fluid in an automatic transmission/transaxle. Describe the specified procedure.

_____

_____

_____ 2. What is the specified fluid required? _____

_____ 3. How many quarts (liters) are required? _____

_____ 4. Check all that apply:

_____ Uses an external filter

_____ Uses an internal filter

_____ Filter is accessible

_____ Transmission/transaxle has a drain plug

_____ Other (specify) _____

_____ 5. Loosen the pan, drain and then remove the transmission/transaxle pan.

_____ 6. Check the bottom of the pan for abnormal (metallic) debris.

_____ OK _____ NOT OK

_____ 7. Install a new gasket, install the pan, torque the fasteners to factory specification.

_____ 8. Install the fluid and check the level.

187

Used Vehicle Inspection

Meets NATEF Task: None Specified

Name _____ **Date** _____

Make/Model _____ **Year** _____ **Instructor's OK** [   ]

_____ **1.** Check the body of the vehicle for evidence of damage or rust.

      ___ Left side   ___**OK**   ___**NOT OK**

      ___ Hood   ___**OK**   ___**NOT OK**

      ___ Roof   ___**OK**   ___**NOT OK**

      ___ Rear/Trunk   ___**OK**   ___**NOT OK**

_____ **2.** Check for proper operation of all doors and windows.

                   ___**OK**   ___**NOT OK**

_____ **3.** Check the condition of all tires, including the spare.   ___**OK**   ___**NOT OK**

_____ **4.** Check that all lights work (interior and exterior).   ___**OK**   ___**NOT OK**

_____ **5.** Check all accessories to make sure they work.   ___**OK**   ___**NOT OK**

_____ **6.** Check all fluids and accessory drive belts.   ___**OK**   ___**NOT OK**

_____ **7.** Start the engine and check for proper operation.   ___**OK**   ___**NOT OK**

_____ **8.** Check online price guides and determine fair market value.

      Fair market value =   _____

      Asking price =   _____

_____ **9.** Would you purchase this vehicle?   ___**YES**   ___**NO**

      Explain why or why not? _____

      _____

      _____

Pre-Delivery Inspection

Meets NATEF Task: None Specified

Name _____ Date _____

Make/Model _____ Year _____ Instructor's OK [   ]

_____ **1.** Carefully inspect the vehicle for damage and document any faults detected.

          ____OK   ____NOT OK _____

_____ **2.** Check the vehicle identification number.

_____ **3.** Remove all exterior protective plastic coverings.

_____ **4.** Remove all interior protective plastic coverings.

_____ **5.** Check the operation of all lights and accessories.

_____ **6.** Check and correct tire inflation pressures.

_____ **7.** Check all fluid levels.

_____ **8.** Check the battery for proper state-of-charge.

_____ **9.** Check the spare tire and jack or inflator unit.

_____ **10.** Start the engine and check for proper operation.

_____ **11.** Use a scan tool and check for any diagnostic trouble codes.

_____ **12.** Test drive the vehicle and check for proper operation, squeaks, or rattles.